PELICAN

AI

ENGLAND

NINETEENTH

DAVID THOMSON

DAVID THOMSON

ENGLAND IN THE NINETEENTH CENTURY

‹ 1815—1914 ›

PENGUIN BOOKS

Penguin Books Ltd, Harmondsworth Middlesex
U.S.A.: Penguin Books Inc., 3300 Clipper Mill Road, Baltimore 11, Md
AUSTRALIA: Penguin Books Pty Ltd, 762, Whitehorse Road,
Mitcham, Victoria

—

First published by Penguin Books 1950
Reprinted 1951, 1953, 1955, 1957

Made and printed in Great Britain
by Hunt, Barnard & Co, Ltd,
Aylesbury

EDITORIAL NOTE

England in the Nineteenth Century is the eighth volume of a series planned to form an intelligent and consecutive guide to the development of English society in all its aspects from the Roman invasion to the outbreak of the first world war. Each volume has been written by a specialist, and each author has been left to decide what he himself considers significant and interesting, in the period with which he deals, and to make his own balance between the claims of the sub-divisions of his general thesis, politics, economics, culture, religion, social life, colonial expansion, foreign relations. All have sought to emphasize the sense of period, and while some parallels are inevitable, the business of discovering comparison and conclusion, and of adapting the lessons of history to our own times, is left, for the most part, to the reader.

The completed series consists of the following eight volumes:

J. E. MORPURGO

CONTENTS

CONTENTS

PREFACE

THIS book is not an attempt to write what is often called a 'general' or 'undifferentiated' history of nineteenth-century England. Still less is it intended as yet another 'text-book' on nineteenth-century England. These tasks have been well performed already. In conformity with the taste and tendency of our times I have tried rather to describe, and as far as possible to explain, the major social changes which the people of England experienced during that remarkable century between 1815 and 1914 which might well be called 'the Great Peace'. In making this attempt we have to draw upon political, economic, intellectual, diplomatic, and any other sort of 'differentiated' or 'specialized' history available to us. But these specialized aspects concern us only in so far as they help to illuminate the changes in mental habit and outlook, or in social life and organization, which constitute the development of the English national community during these years. Since actual wars play so small a part in the period with which we are concerned it has not been felt necessary to supply details about the battles of Inkerman or Balaclava, Omdurman or Majuba Hill: though in the history of England before 1815 or after 1914 military details might appropriately be given. Similarly, even social history itself has not been regarded as concerned primarily with the invention of sulphur matches or cheap soap, though both these belong to the period, and are in themselves momentous contributions to human comfort. The aim has been to paint the main outlines with a broad brush, and to introduce as much factual detail, but no more, plundered from the whole of history within the period, as is necessary to demonstrate the nature, inter-connexions, and significance of the social changes described.

The main *motif* of the period, as I understand it, is the remarkable accumulation of material wealth and power which the English people achieved during the century. In examining how this wealth and power were accumulated and whence they derived we are led also to consider how they were used and how they eventually diminished. For much of the time Englishmen were unconscious of many of the very foundations of this power. The world-wide power of the City of London, for example, was as discreetly veiled from public view as the legs of mid-Victorian pianos; the supremacy of the British Navy was normally as silent as footsteps upon the layers of drawing-room carpets. And, because the nakedness of power was withheld from view, men for long periods forgot how necessary this basis of power was to the whole structure of English greatness. It was, paradoxically, when this power was crumbling that Englishmen began to talk about it – and even to brandish it – most. But even when least fully aware of whence their power came Victorian Englishmen usually used it well, for they used it in the cause of freedom: again, it was when they became more fully conscious of it, and when it was declining, that they more often used it ill. If the problem of power – now atomic as well as economic – is the prime issue of our times, it may be that we can learn some wisdom from the strange drama of Victorian England.

D. T.

Sidney Sussex College
  Cambridge
    April 1950

CHAPTER I

BRITAIN IN 1815

The Social Scene

WHAT was Great Britain like when she won the battle of Waterloo? She was a country of some 13 million people – roughly a quarter of her present population. This number was fast increasing, and by 1871 it had doubled. The chief reasons for this quick growth were simple enough. They were that more babies survived and that Englishmen were living longer. Even in the slums of the new industrial towns expectation of life was better than ever before. People were already, on the whole, better fed, better clothed, less likely to contract disease and better cared for when they did, than during the eighteenth century. A further reason for the growth of population was that Irish immigrants were pouring into western England and Scotland, though soon Irish, Scots, and English were to reverse this direction of emigration and flock westwards towards North America.

Most Englishmen in 1815 still worked on the land or in trades connected with agriculture, though within the next generation most Englishmen became townsmen engaged in industry: sixteen years after Waterloo probably half the population already lived under urban conditions. Large urban populations were gathering in the north-west of England, in South Wales, and between the Firth of Forth and the Firth of Clyde. During the first thirty years of the century Birmingham and Sheffield doubled in size, Liverpool, Leeds, Manchester, and Glasgow more than doubled. London, in 1815, was above the million mark, and five years later numbered 1,274,000.

These urban populations were still mostly country-bred, with the traditional outlook and character of country folk. Their children, too often reared in the slum-conditions which resulted from the shoddy houses rushed up to accommodate the newcomers, were a new social phenomenon in the northern towns. In the eighteenth century a few big towns – mostly ports like London, Bristol, and Liverpool – had their town-bred and even slum-bred populations, brutalized by ignorance, squalor, and the habits of gin-drinking. The city mob had been a fearsome terror to governments during the second half of the century. Now this old evil assumed vaster proportions, and with the increasing employment of women and children in the coal-mines of Wales or the unhealthy cotton-mills of Lancashire, great new social problems were created. William Cobbett deplored the 'oatmeal and water' diet of these folk uprooted from the soil.

> If, when I go to the north, I find the labourers *eating more meat* than those of the 'sooth', I shall then say that 'enlightening' is a very good thing; but give me none of that 'light', or of that 'grace', which makes a man content with oatmeal and water, or that makes him lie down and die of starvation amidst abundance of food . . . Talk of *vassals!* Talk of *villains!* Talk of *serfs!* Are there any of these, or did feudal times ever see any of them, so debased, so absolutely slaves, as the poor creatures who, in the 'enlightened' north, are compelled to work fourteen hours a day, in a heat of eighty-four degrees, and who are liable to punishment for looking out at a window of the factory!

At the time of Waterloo, therefore, Britain was midway through the most far-reaching social transformation in her whole history. Her industrial heart was beginning to throb, first in the great cotton-mills of Lancashire and soon in her coal-mines and blast-furnaces. From America came raw cotton to be spun and woven, mainly by steam-driven machinery in mills or factories which were privately owned and which employed hundreds of men, women, and children. Already, in 1815, her import of cotton amounted to 82 million pounds; and by 1860 it rose to 1000 million pounds. The wool industry, her traditional staple industry for export, was undergoing more slowly a similar transformation. Power spinning was driving out hand spinning, but weaving factories were not established on a big scale until a generation later. Next in importance to these textile industries were the heavy industries of iron, coal, and engineering. The wars just ended had brought a boom to them, and the great age of railways which began in the 1830s turned them into one of the chief sources of national wealth. Already the inventions of Joseph Bramah, Henry Maudslay, and others had laid the basis of big engineering firms; and in a few years the making of machine-tools – machines which made machines – introduced a new phase of the industrial revolution. In transport, the network of canals was nearly complete before Waterloo, and the main roads were being remade by Thomas Telford and John McAdam.

So the survivors of the 30,000 British men who fought the battle of Waterloo returned to a country that was fast changing its very appearance, and whose wealth was rapidly increasing by reason of new methods of manufacture and transport. But still the factory areas were a small part of the whole, and most English towns were picturesque country towns, set in a countryside of unspoilt beauty. The villages, to which most of them came home, were still the main focus of life for most Englishmen, and had almost completed their eighteenth-century transformation. The countryside was now drained, ditched, hedged, and en-

closed to an extent that would have amazed their grand-
fathers. Nearly all the old open fields had been enclosed;
and the commons and waste lands had been enclosed nearly
as much as they were ever to be. This meant that agriculture had become more efficient. Improved methods of
tilling, of rotation of crops, and of stock-breeding had become well known, even if they were not yet universally
adopted by the farmers. It also meant that more of the land
was now owned by wealthy men, who let it to tenant-
farmers; many of the old smallholders had become landless, agricultural labourers or else had drifted into the new
towns. Cottagers had in most cases lost their old common
rights, and the fuel they used to gather from the waste lands,
and their diet was more often than not bread and cheese for
six days in the week. The luckier ones had small gardens in
which they grew vegetables, or kept a pig and a few fowls.
Six years after Waterloo that sturdy, blustering countryman
William Cobbett mounted his horse and began his famous
'Rural Rides' through the shires of England. He found
plenty of occasions to lament the sufferings and injustices of
the disinherited poor. He noted that

> There is one farmer, in the North of Hampshire, who has nearly
> eight thousand acres of land in his hands; who grows fourteen
> hundred acres of wheat and two thousand acres of barley! He
> occupies what was formerly 40 farms! Is it any wonder that *paupers
> increase?*

Like many spokesmen of the old 'agricultural interest' in his
day, he deplored the rise of a new, more irresponsible, and
purely profit-making class of landed gentry which had
drawn its wealth from trade and finance. He never tired of
pointing out

> the difference between a resident *native* gentry, attached to the soil,
> known to every farmer and labourer from their childhood, fre-
> quently mixing with them in those pursuits where all artificial dis-
> tinctions are lost, practising hospitality without ceremony, from

habit and not on calculation; and a gentry only now-and-then residing at all, having no relish for country-delights, foreign in their manners, distant and haughty in their behaviour, looking to the soil only for its rents, viewing it as a mere object of speculation, unacquainted with its cultivators, despising them and their pursuits, and relying, for influence, not upon the good will of the vicinage, but upon the dread of their power. The war and paper-system has brought in nabobs, negro-drivers, generals, admirals, governors, commissaries, contractors, pensioners, sinecurists, commissioners, loan-jobbers, lottery-dealers, bankers, stock-jobbers; not to mention the long and *black list* in gowns and three-tailed wigs. You can see but few good houses not in possession of one or the other of these. These, with the parsons, are now the magistrates.

The outcry against the 'Nabobs' of the East India Company and the stock-holders of the national debt was a very old one, and Cobbett was seldom averse to exaggeration: even allowing for these facts, here was a new wealthy class which was gathering up great riches and power into its hands, and which betokened great social changes yet to come.

Both old and new landed gentry were certainly wealthy, happy, and engrossed in the life of their pleasant and beautiful country houses. The war had scarcely upset the delightful routine of their lives. Even the seven campaigns of the Pensinular War against Napoleon – the period of Britain's greatest expeditionary forces to the continent – cost less than 40,000 British lives. Both rents and tithes had risen with the price of corn, and the income tax was more tiresome than burdensome to the landed gentry. The labouring and manufacturing classes suffered from the dearness of corn and the periodic economic crises. The growing habit, which came to be known as the 'Speenhamland system', of paying poor relief to supplement wages, helped them to evade starvation, at least in the southern counties. This practice, which in the short run benefited the working classes but in the long run pauperized and demoralized them, certainly benefited the large employing farmer. It relieved him from the need to pay his workmen a living wage, and forced the small independent parish ratepayer to contribute, via the poor rate, to the wages bill of the big farmer and the big manufacturer. By 1818 – the peak year for poor relief – the sum so spent amounted to £8 millions.

These were, perhaps, the most striking features of the English social scene in 1815. As usual, the new forces tended to attract attention and got exaggerated. Cobbett often noted with pleasure that village labourers fared well in some districts, and that small independent farmers still flourished. From Burlip Hill he looked across the Vale of Gloucester and saw that

> All here is fine; fine farms; fine pastures; all inclosed fields; all divided by hedges; orchards a plenty; and I had scarcely seen one apple since I left Berkshire. Gloucester is a fine, clean, beautiful place; and, which is of a vast deal more importance, the labourers' dwellings, as I came along, looked good, and the labourers themselves pretty well as to dress and healthiness.

In Sussex he noted that

> There is an appearance of comfort about the dwellings of the labourers, all along here, that is very pleasant to behold. The gardens are neat, and full of vegetables of the best kinds. I see very few of 'Ireland's lazy root' . . . I saw, and with great delight, a pig at almost every labourer's house. The houses are good and warm; and the gardens some of the best that I have ever seen in England.

A few years later it was revealed, in the census of 1831, that nearly a million families were engaged in agriculture, of which 145,000 were those of owners or farmers who hired no labour, as against 686,000 families of labourers who worked for wages. The small yeoman farmer had been declining in numbers before 1780; and although he became more common again after 1780 he became more and more of a rarity after 1832. In 1830 the starving field labourers of the southern counties rioted in support of their demand for a wage of half-a-crown a day. Three of them were hanged and 420 were deported to Australia: which serves to emphasize a different aspect of social life at this time – the savagery of the laws and the penalties to which the working classes were subjected.

There were some 220 offences for which the death penalty could be imposed: and although it was not often exacted, because judges had consciences and juries might refuse to convict, the iniquitous criminal code was a standing menace to the happiness and security of the people. Seven years before Waterloo Samuel Romilly persuaded the House of Commons to accept transportation for life, instead of hanging, as the punishment for pickpockets: when, in the course of the next few years, he tried several times to get the repeal of an old statute which permitted the death penalty for the theft of five shillings from a shop, he was regularly defeated by the House of Lords. Other capital offences ranged from highway robbery and murder to such curious crimes as injuring Westminster Bridge or impersonating out-pensioners of Chelsea Hospital. It was 1832 before housebreaking, sheep-stealing, and forgery ceased to be in the list: but after 1838, no one was hanged except for murder or attempted murder. In 1815 it was the game laws which were the most burdensome and dangerous legal hardship for the working classes, and they were as much a sign of the continued ascendancy of the landowners as was the protective corn-law of 1815 itself. It was illegal for anyone to buy or sell game, which put much money into the pockets of professional poachers; it was illegal for anyone who was not the squire or a squire's eldest son to kill game. The cottager caught with his nets at night, in quest of a hare or rabbit, could by a new law of 1816 be transported for seven years. Pheasant preserves could be protected by spring-guns and mantraps, and the practice was upheld by the law courts until 1827. A 'poaching war' was carried on between gentry and gamekeepers on one side, and gangs of armed thugs, often from the towns, on the other; and it was evidence that they produced disorder, as much as that they produced hardship, which led to the gradual repeal of the game laws.

London, by reason of being the capital and of its particular concentration of population, produced immediately after Waterloo a very special problem of crime. Contemporaries believed that the peace, demobilization, and post-war distress produced a great increase in crime. In 1816 there was set up a Committee on the Police of the Metropolis which investigated the situation. It was very searching in its inquiries but concluded that crimes were 'much less atrocious than formerly'. In fact, what had changed was people's attitude to crime and public order, comparable with the changed attitude to the penal code. The nature and purpose of crime was changing, but not for the worse. Increased convictions did not signify increased crime. The condition of London has been summed up like this:

> London to a great extent escaped both the torrent of pauperiza-tion which deluged the greater part of agricultural England, and the catastrophic fall in wages which occurred in many places . . . The transition from war to peace undoubtedly brought much misery and unemployment, it was a shrinkage from a period of commercial and industrial expansion under war conditions – a period of chequered and hectic prosperity. But in spite of this, there is much evidence against a general set-back in social conditions in London . . . Foreign-ers generally comment on the sturdy, well-dressed appearance of working people. Doctors testify to the improvement in health and cleanliness. There was much poverty, but it was being more com-prehensively dealt with by the poor laws and by charities than ever before. The death rate for London as for the whole country con-tinued to decline. (M. D. George: *London Life in the XVIIIth Century*, p. 18f.)

The same historian of the capital points out that hardships begin to be talked about only when they are no longer taken for granted: and it is the increased attention paid to them that is perhaps the main feature of the period that opens in 1815. Sweated labour and cellar dwellings were not invented by the men who made the industrial revolution: they were discovered by them, discussed by them, and in the end partially remedied by them.

London, of course, had its other side. In the days of the Regency it became, even more conspicuously than usual, the centre of fashion. And of what fashions! It was the age of the dandies and their feminine counterparts the dandizette, with their exaggeratedly foppish costumes and habits; of Beau Brummell and the popularity of Brighton; of dignified gentlemen flying along the roads on their hobby-horses – a new craze which was a cross between a scooter and a bicycle, propelled by the feet on the ground. Miss Jane Austen and Sir Walter Scott were bringing out their oddly contrasted novels, but the most eagerly-awaited news of the day for most people was the results of the horse races and the prize fights. The popularity of the prize fight has been well described by Professor Trevelyan.

> When the date and place of a prize-fight had been announced, hordes set out, driving, riding, and walking to the spot from all parts of the island. Sometimes twenty thousand spectators assembled. In one aspect these vast outdoor assemblies were festivals of the common people. But the priests of the national cult were fashionable members of the aristocracy, who presided over the ceremonies and held the rough and often turbulent multitude in awe. It was these men of fashion and rank who hired and backed the gladiators . . . Their lordly patrons were proud to be seen driving with them to the ring-side in coach or gig. (*English Social History*, p. 503.)

However widely divided by rank and wealth Englishmen might be, at least they were apt to meet round the ring-side of Belcher, Tom Cribb, or Tom Spring.

The Political Scene

Such was the England of Waterloo. How was she governed? Her king was the aged George III, who had begun his reign with ambitious plans in 1760, only to run into the most serious opposition that any government of England had met with since the days of the great Revolution of 1688. This opposition had come at first from the great Whig landowning families – the Newcastles, Rockinghams, Temples – which had ruled England in the days of the first two Georges. By attacking their oligarchic power and resuming into his own hands many of the royal powers which his predecessors had allowed to slip from them George had aroused the bitter enmity of the aristocracy. He had driven some of them to form an alliance – however uncomfortable and unusual they might feel in it – with more plebeian elements in the English population. Men of the middle-classes like Edmund Burke, the Irish lawyer, had been found to phrase, in golden and memorable words, the great protest of the Whigs against royal domination of Parliament. Mischievous adventurers like John Wilkes, who gained the loyalty of the discontented lower-middle classes and the town-mobs, had devised new methods of popular agitation, through big-scale associations, public meetings, and organized petitions to Parliament and the King. Above all the American colonists, greatly roused by the inconsistent and often vexatious policies of the King and his Ministers as regards taxation, had ventured on open rebellion which the British Government found itself unable to check. The result was the loss of the American colonies to the Crown, and the creation of a new independent American Union across the Atlantic. This blow, the greatest that royal prestige had suffered, had been followed by the long and costly French wars. The King himself, suffering from recurrent fits of

madness, in 1811 had to give way to the permanent
Regency of his son, the disreputable and somewhat ludicrous
George IV. So apart from popular sympathy roused by the
spectacle of the old and ailing monarch, the kingship of
Britain was at a very low ebb.

Power and prestige which the monarchy had lost, Parliament, and the Prime Ministers whose power rested on
parliamentary support, had gained. The younger William
Pitt, national hero of the French wars, had died in 1806.
His successors as Prime Ministers were less heroic figures,
and in 1815 the holder of the office was the liberal-minded
and unspectacular Lord Liverpool He for the next twelve
years presided over a mixed cabinet of men harassed by
post-war problems, frightened of the spread of French
'Jacobinism' amongst the discontented classes of England,
and varying in policy between savage repression in time of
scares, and mild, piecemeal reforms in the face of severe discontent. Political parties were still led by the aristocracy and
gentry of England, with a gentle admixture of spokesmen of
the rising business, commercial, and manufacturing interests. They were acquiring better organization inside Parliament, but still – save in a few precocious constituencies –
lacked that network of local party committees and associations which their successors in the mid-Victorian age were
to build up everywhere in the country. The country gentry,
as squires and Justices of the Peace, were still the real
governors of the countryside.

The antiquated electoral system on which Parliament
rested was made more than ever out of date by the growth
and shift of population and the rise of large northern towns.
The franchise in the counties – freeholders of land worth
forty shillings a year – gave the vote to most of the well-to-do farmers and most of the smaller landowners. The
franchise in the boroughs varied enormously, but in few

save the larger towns of London, Westminster, and Bristol was it in any way representative of the population. Such voters as there were treated the vote as a property-right, to be sold at elections to the highest bidder, or given automatically for the traditional landowner who regarded the boroughs on his land as 'in his pocket'. Although it was uncommon for many seats to be contested, even at times of general elections, there was already a tendency for more and more to be contested; which was a sign that public opinion was taking shape about certain political and social issues, and that people felt strongly enough about politics to vote more according to conscience than to custom. Yet it is a little anachronistic to speak of the Commons of 1815 as 'unreformed'. The prevailing eighteenth-century theory still held the ground – that it is property and not people which ought to be represented in Parliament. Only the growing movements of Radicals held that men should have votes as men and as citizens, and not as the owners of specified quantities of landed property. And Radicals, for the moment, were associated with Jacobins – the revolutionaries of France who had brought war to England and so much misery to Europe.

As for the House of Lords – the other half of Britain's Parliament – that had recently undergone considerable change, which was not necessarily reform. One sign of the change wrought by the reign of George III was that the traditional stronghold of the Whig landed aristocracy had become a Tory stronghold. Pitt's period of premiership had seen 109 new peerages created, and the nineteenth-century House of Lords started 50 per cent larger in size than the normal eighteenth-century House had been. Lord Liverpool added another fifty-six. Peerages were becoming the normal method of royal reward for services rendered and the regular way of ensuring governmental influence, since so many

sinecure offices had been abolished at the end of the eighteenth century. A pamphleteer of 1795, describing *How to
make a Peer*, wrote:

> Take a man, with or without parts, of an ancient or a new family,
> with one or two boroughs at his command, previous to a dissolu-
> tion. Let him renounce all former professions or obligations, and
> engage to bring in your friends and support yourself.

From being a small and select family party of oligarchic
leaders, the House had become more broadly representative
of the whole nation and more comparable in size with the
Commons. It now numbered some 360 members, some of
them distinguished generals and admirals, some merchants,
brewers, and manufacturers. Since Peers normally out-
numbered commoners in the Cabinet, this was a most
important development in the government of England.

The political parties, thrown into some confusion of
principles and sentiments by their various reactions to the
French Revolution and the Napoleonic wars during the
period 1789–1815, had not yet taken the clear shape they
were to assume in the days of Gladstone and Disraeli. The
Tory Party was little more than the union of all men and
groups who regarded Jacobinism as something to be resisted
and destroyed. Under the inspiration of Pitt and Edmund
Burke, whose *Reflections on the Revolution in France* of 1790
became the bible of Conservatism, the Tory Party had
become identified with total opposition to movements of
popular radicalism and political reform. It remained the
party of the Church of England, of public order and administrative efficiency, of continuity and traditionalism in
methods of government. It clung to a hierarchical and
aristocratic notion of society, later to be embodied in the
mid-Victorian doctrine of 'the rich man in his castle, the
poor man at his gate.' The Whigs, in so far as they were
still led by men like Grey and Russell, shared in much of

this outlook; but in so far as they were supported by the Protestant Dissenters, the moneyed men of the City, the fundholders of the Bank, and many of the rising merchant and manufacturing interests, they sought gradual reform of the system of government, of financial and commercial policy, and of the social and legal system. They wanted to lessen the old power and privileges of the landed interest. Lord Brougham, in 1816, was not afraid to adopt something of the Radical technique of popular agitation, with its frequent county and parish meetings.

It was the Radical movements which set the pace in effective political organization, and which were soon to dominate the whole growth of British parliamentarianism. At Oldham, Middleton, and Manchester 'Union' societies were formed in 1816, drawing their support from the industrial areas of Lancashire and conducting agitation against the Corn Laws – especially the Law of 1815. They denounced it as keeping bread dear for the benefit of the landowners and farmers. They quickly joined hands with the 'Hampden Clubs', founded during the war by the veteran Radical agitator Major John Cartwright. Under the leadership of Sir Francis Burdett and the popular orator Hunt they organized mass meetings, debates, and petitions to Parliament much as the radical movements of the days of Wilkes had done. Soon their work was shared with a series of political journalists and pamphleteers – Thomas Wooler in his *Black Dwarf* (1817–24), Richard Carlile and his *Republican* (1819–26), and the redoubtable William Cobbett in his *Political Register*. Here was the fountain-head of that mighty stirring of public opinion and that series of dynamic popular movements which were to provide the driving-power for so many of the reforms achieved during the century.

It would be misleading to draw over-sharp lines of distinction between the three main bodies of opinion which can too glibly be labelled 'Tory', 'Whig', and 'Radical' in 1815. Lord Liverpool, George Canning, and William Huskisson, who ranked officially as 'Tory Ministers', shaded imperceptibly in outlook and policy into the more conservative wing of the Whigs. They were as ready for limited free-trade measures as Grey or Russell. So, too, the more progressive 'Whigs' such as Sheridan, Whitbread, Tierney, and the younger supporters were ready for almost as much political and social reform as the 'Tory-Radical' Cobbett. Even in this time of deep division of opinion and widespread social distress the shades of English politics were subtle and gentle and merged easily one into one another. The Tories, who had led the country in the long war against Napoleon's domination of Europe and who in the process had been led to support insurgent nationalist and even liberal movements abroad, were unlikely to be so adamant in their hostility to the ideals of liberal nationalism as they had been in the days of Pitt or Burke. Just as the French Revolution had helped to liberalize the Whigs, because their younger leaders such as Charles James Fox welcomed it, so Napoleon had unwittingly helped to liberalize the Tories. Only the extremes of each party – Lord Eldon and the Duke of Wellington at one extreme, the Union and Hampden Clubs at the other – tended to speak and think in the more bitter terms of 1793.

The International Scene

Britain, as one of the victorious Powers which had defeated the great Napoleon, held a high place in international councils after Waterloo. The most persistent and invulnerable of his enemies, she had defeated him at sea and joined with Russia and Prussia in defeating him on land. Her population was less than half that of France, barely half Austria's, and only a little more than Prussia's. By her combination of commercial and naval power she had defeated equally his attempts to blockade her and his preparations to invade her: and unlike most European countries she ended the war unravaged and unoccupied by the troops of the *Grande Armée*.

Her power rested less on the amount of available manpower, and more on her superiority in industrial and commercial technique, and on her degree of national unity at a time when Germany was splintered into a couple of dozen small States and Italy into half a dozen, when eastern Europe was still almost entirely agricultural and ruled by reactionary dynastic monarchs, and when Russia, Britain's most serious rival in the Near East, was excluded from far-reaching influence in Europe by the barrier of the Prussian State and the Habsburg and Turkish Empires. After the defeat of France Britain remained the greatest Power in western Europe and the Mediterranean, and, despite the loss of America, supreme in the colonial world of North America, the West Indies, and India. The markets of the world lay wide open to her manufactured goods, and the undeveloped areas of the globe to her capital investments. Soon the City of London became the economic capital of the world.

This was the greatest opportunity in Britain's history. Her enormous economic advantages, skilfully and opportunely used, could bring her a prosperity and a kind of world-leadership hitherto unknown. To her merchants, bankers, and manufacturers, eager to avail themselves of these golden opportunities, only two great obstacles seemed likely to hamper their activities. One was the set of restrictions imposed upon their free and plentiful import of raw materials by the Corn Laws and Navigation Acts. The other was the feudal and monarchical reaction in Europe, led by Austria and Russia. This was calculated to drag Europe – and with it the overseas possessions of Spain and Portugal – back to the old order of feudal and clerical privilege and dynastic imperialism which represented all that was most hostile to the free-trading, competitive, highly capitalistic spirit of Britain's merchants and manufacturers. The open door for migration, capital investment, and markets was the essential demand for British shippers, factory-owners, and financiers in the nineteenth century. It was the creed natural to any people which has great natural advantages and a long lead in methods of production. Free competition is of most value to those who need not fear any competition.

Already, too, the general spirit of the country backed this policy. As a constitutional parliamentary Monarchy, however great its defects judged by modern democratic standards, Britain of 1815 enjoyed a system of government more enlightened, tolerant, and capable of peaceful reform than any other major power in Europe. Even her Tory ministries soon found the Holy Alliance of European Emperors, the Congress System set up by the Congress of Vienna which made the peace-settlement with France, and the policies of repression shaped by the Austrian Chancellor Prince Metternich, far too restrictive and oppressive for her purposes. First among the important victorious Powers, she broke with the System and thereby made it crumble. Her foreign policy henceforth was concerned with the defence of her colonial territories, systematic resistance to Russian expansion towards the Balkans and the Mediterranean, and the restoration of good relationships with France. A succession of great foreign ministers, from Castlereagh, Canning, and Palmerston to Disraeli and Salisbury, developed a characteristically free-handed British foreign policy which rested on these basic aims.

It was not only the goods, gold, and men that Britain sent out into the world that made her a great Power after Waterloo. It was also the ideas and ideals which she absorbed into herself that made her a leader of world opinion. England enjoyed the stirring of intellect and conscience which came with the tide of democratic ideals derived from the American and French Revolutions. These ideas – of the natural right of all men to liberty, equality, and the pursuit of happiness – could be slowly absorbed into her national traditions and the working of her national institutions: slowly, and all the more beneficially, because she did not suffer the impact of these great upheavals within her own body as did America and France. The tide in both instances struck England externally, and glanced off her because she was engaged in resisting the revolutions to which it gave rise in America and France. Because her political institutions were spared this shock, they could assimilate the nourishing and stimulating ideas of democracy in an almost pre-digested form, and could avoid most of the excesses and violent disturbances which racked her neighbours. Her parliamentary system, being more flexible and adjustable than the monarchical regimes of the continent, could be gradually adapted to meet the needs of the more refined and assimilable versions of democracy which became conceivable after the experience of France. It could 'broaden down from precedent to precedent', making England in the process the most ingeniously inventive nation in the nineteenth century in the art of politics. Thus it was that the devices of representative parliamentary government, the party and cabinet systems, ministerial political responsibility, and the permanent civil service, were all – in their familiar modern forms at least – the inventions of nineteenth-century England. All were devised in the effort to reconcile institutions resting on the theory of the 'sovereignty of Parliament' with movements demanding the 'sovereignty of the people'. In a similar way, Britain so successfully applied the lessons learnt from the loss of America that she devised, through the conception of responsible colonial government, the notion and reality of 'Dominion status', which have created a structure of Empire unique in the history of the world. Foreign ideas, like her foreign cotton, she contrived to import, transform into articles more valuable and finished, and to export at a profit after satisfying her own needs at home.

This political inventiveness, no less than her mechanical inventiveness, brought her great prestige abroad. Suppressed nationalities in eastern Europe, liberal and even socialistic movements in western Europe, learned to look to England for leadership, protection, or in the last resort refuge. Other countries, envious of her success in combining democracy with stability, and self-government with responsibility, tended to imitate her parliamentary form of government just as they borrowed her industrial techniques and skills. But machinery and factory-plant proved often to be more transplantable than political institutions. If the first period of our study, between 1815 and 1850, saw the growth of liberal and democratic movements in Europe partly under stimulus of Britain's example, the second period, between 1851 and 1874, saw the defeat of most of these movements and the reversion to more dictatorial and anti-democratic regimes. Meanwhile the more successful imitation of British industrial methods brought increased resources of power and wealth to these new regimes, with the result that in the last quarter of the century Britain found herself threatened by severe economic competitors and by powerful political rivals in the continent of Europe. Above all Germany, unified politically by the undemocratic methods of Bismarck and industrialized by the intensive exploitation of the coal and iron resources of Alsace-Lorraine, the Ruhr, and Silesia, confronted her as a rival which she had twice to defeat, in world wars of the present century, before even her national security could be assured.

Philosophical Radicalism, or 'Benthamism' as it is more usually called after its founder, Jeremy Bentham (1748–1832), was the most characteristic intellectual product of England at this period. Bentham and his followers such as James Mill (1773–1836), his son John Stuart Mill (1806–73), and Edwin Chadwick (1800–90) dominated English Radical thought throughout the century. Starting from the belief that men are prompted in their behaviour by the desire to seek pleasure and to avoid pain, and that the purpose of all legislation should be to promote 'the greatest happiness of the greatest number', Bentham founded a school of thought which, developing and changing in the hands of his disciples as the century progressed, provided a dynamic force of legal, social, political, and economic reform, and a touchstone for all governmental policies. The movement began by adopting completely the *laissez-faire*, individualistic doctrines of Adam Smith (1723–90) in economics, and a far-reaching programme of legal simplification and codification which in time transformed the whole system of English common law and judicial procedure. Although identified at first with opposition to all State interference in economic and social life and a distrust of all positive efforts of governments to do good to their subjects, it was transformed by the force of circumstances and by the inherent implications of its central social doctrine – 'the greatest happiness of the greatest number' – into a philosophy of legislative reform, social-service organization, and even a variety of Socialism.

Hitherto the three chief functions of the State had been simply the securing of national defence, the maintaining of public order, and the protection of property. From Tudor times and even from the seventeenth century had come down a legacy of attempts at paternalist interference in such matters as poor relief, foreign trade, and the protection of agriculture. Most of these were by now out of date or inoperative, and Bentham conceived it as his job to strip the statute-book of all such legal relics. The less law the more liberty, and if only the State would leave people alone they would, by the pursuit of their own interests, automatically promote the greatest happiness of the greatest number. He was not entirely consistent, for he admitted the need of good laws to prevent people from harming one another in political and social life, while he denied the need for similar State-action in economic life. He posed a social question – 'What is the common good?' He gave a social answer – 'The greatest happiness of the greatest number!' But he thought that this good would be attained if the State would confine itself to its minimum traditional functions and leave all the rest to the 'invisible hand' of providence which ensured that each man, seeking his own pleasure or profit, would automatically promote the general good and the general profit. This very negative interpretation of his own principle was inadequate. It soon became glaringly inadequate in the conditions of early Victorian England. His principle was capable of much wider and more positive interpretation, permitting of very extensive State action. It was Bentham's disciples, Mill and Chadwick, who saw this and built on it the liberal philosophy of social reform.

Men learned to look to Britain for world leadership not only because she held the secret of economic prosperity and the key to political stability, but also because she seemed to have discovered the philosophy of happiness. Some of her leading statesmen were inspired with the passion to spread these threefold blessings to all mankind: and they identified free trade and parliamentary government with universal happiness and peace. Richard Cobden (1804–65), her leading apostle and missionary of free trade, looked at it like this:

> Commerce is the grand panacea, which, like a beneficent medical discovery, will serve to inoculate with the healthy and saving taste for civilization all the nations of the world. Not a bale of merchandise leaves our shores, but it bears the seeds of intelligence and fruitful thought to the members of some less enlightened community; not a merchant visits our seats of manufacturing industry, but he returns to his own country the missionary of freedom, peace, and good government – while our steam boats, that now visit every port of Europe, and our miraculous railroads, that are the talk of all nations, are the advertisements and vouchers for the value of our enlightened institutions.

The Victorian Adventure

For all these reasons, England in 1815 was on the brink of an era of prosperity and greatness unrivalled in her whole history. The use she made of these great advantages is one theme of her history which calls for study. At the same time, she was entering upon a period of remarkable social distress and unrest, of economic crisis and political change. Her new wealth and her world supremacy rested on foundations of harsh sweated labour, appalling slum conditions in her new towns, and immense human misery. Progress and the enlightenment of which Cobden was so proud coincided with conditions of cut-throat competition and inhuman exploitation: and much of her subsequent history has been the story of successive but not always successful efforts to reconcile her ideals of political democracy and universal happiness with the realities of economic distress and oppression. To bridge this enormous gulf she gradually devised the complex apparatus of the modern social-service State, with its ideals of full employment, social security, and freedom from fear and from want. To succeed in this task was the greatest challenge of all to her political and social inventiveness. But the main advance in this direction came after 1914.

To sum up. The generation of Englishmen between 1815 and 1850 suffered from the combined aftermath of two great social and political revolutions, the American and the French; of two great social and economic upheavals, the agrarian and the industrial revolutions; of two great foreign wars, the French Revolutionary and the Napoleonic Wars (1793–1815). The American and French Revolutions set in motion a whole tide of new forces and ideas in politics, and these seeped gradually into her national life after 1815. The agrarian and industrial revolutions, already well advanced before 1815, transformed the face and life of the nation and brought immense prosperity and misery combined. The French Revolutionary and Napoleonic Wars cut right across the effects of both these other events, speeding industrialization but retarding social and political reforms, crushing England's chief continental rival while they liberalized her own politics, and establishing Britain as the peer of great imperial dynasties such as the Habsburgs of Austria and the Romanovs of Russia. It is not surprising that the period of our study is one of strenuous activity and dynamic change, of ferment of ideas and recurrent social unrest, of great inventiveness and expansion. The whole meaning of Victorian England is lost if it is thought of as a country of stuffy complacency and black top-hatted moral priggery. Its frowsty crinolines and dingy hansom-cabs, its gas-lit houses and over-ornate draperies, concealed a people engaged in a tremendously exciting adventure – the daring experiment of fitting industrial man into a democratic society. Their failures, faults, and ludicrous shortcomings are all too apparent: but the days when Mr Lytton Strachey could afford to laugh at the foibles of the 'Eminent Victorians' have passed, and we must ask ourselves the question whether we *can* laugh at our great-grandfathers' attempts to solve problems to which we have so far failed to find an answer. At least the Victorians found greatness, stability, and peace: and the whole world, marvelling, envied them for it.

CHAPTER II

THE FORCES OF CHANGE

Conflicting Interests

DURING the great wars agriculture in England had enjoyed a boom. The improving landlords of the period – such as Coke of Norfolk (1752–1842), who spent half a million pounds on his estate and raised his annual rental from just over £2000 to some £20,000 – enjoyed a big increase in rents during the Napoleonic Wars. Arthur Young (1741–1820) waged a campaign against the waste lands and the open-fields system with its scattered strips. In large districts wastes, open fields, and commons had been steadily enclosed during the eighteenth century, and inside the enclosures more scientific farming, better stock-breeding, and agricultural experiments could be carried out. The result was more corn grown; it was also the dispossession of the small-holder and the independent yeomen farmers, the destruction of communal rights and consequent poverty for the cottar who had lived on the margin of subsistence, the creation of a large landless labourer class uprooted from the soil and forced either to work for a wage or wander into the new towns. The farmers grew corn in a big way to feed England during the wars: but they often cultivated chalk lands or moorlands that were normally uneconomic to use for corn, and after the wars when the price of corn fell they demanded protection.

Accordingly, in 1815, Parliament passed a Corn Law which prohibited the import of corn until the price on the home market reached eighty shillings a quarter. This, it was hoped, would keep up the price of corn sold by English farmers, ensure stability and profits to landlord, farmer, and labourer alike, and tide over the period of transition from war to peace. It was something of a panic measure, for the immediate results of the drop of prices after the war had been a drop in rents, frequent bankruptcies, and unemployment in the countryside. Demobilized soldiers added to the supply of labour available just when less labour was called for on the farms. The Corn Law was the wrong answer to a real economic problem, and until the middle of the century farmers were in almost constant distress. Because it made bread dear, poorer people could not afford to buy bacon, eggs, cheese, butter, milk, beer, meat, and all other farm products. So even when corn fetched good prices, farming as a whole did not flourish. Further, the Corn Law led to disastrous fluctuations in prices, because when the harvest was bad and prices rose high, the dealers rushed in corn from abroad and prices suddenly slumped. This instability caused hardships not only to the farmers themselves, but to the urban populations whose wages remained more steady and at a low level. In 1828 an experiment was made with a new Corn Law, designed to give more stability. On paper it was ingenious enough. It fixed a sliding scale of import duties, so that high duties replaced total prohibition when home prices were low, and were gradually lowered as home prices rose. It was hoped that this would encourage the gradual importation of corn as the import duties fell, and so keep the home supply at a steady level. The scheme reckoned without the dealers and speculators in the corn-trade, who tended to store their imported corn in bonded warehouses until the duty fell as low as it was likely to be, and then flooded the market with their imported corn just when the home prices were reaching their peak. The result was again sudden slumps in prices with the sudden gluts on the market, and the new Corn Law worked no better than the old.

The use to which the landed interests put their pre-dominance in Parliament to protect themselves in this way at the expense of the industrial populations of the towns and the manufacturing interests caused the first big open split between landed and manufacturing interests. All alike wanted steady and level prices: but the industrial interests, employers and workers alike, wanted this to be a low level, so as to make wages go further, keep wage-bills low and therefore the cost of manufactured goods low, and enable them to reap maximum benefits in world markets. The cotton-merchants likewise wanted the plentiful import of cheap corn to enable the corn-exporting countries to pay for the manufactured cotton goods that England exported. The landowners and farmers wanted corn-prices stabilized at a high level. Thus two distinct groups of economic interest grew up, bitterly hostile to one another: and this led to the long agitation for the repeal of the Corn Laws, the Free Trade movement as a whole, and the demand for the lessen-ing of the power enjoyed by the agricultural and landed interests in Parliament.

Another conflict of social and economic interests was be-coming manifest, which cut across this battle between landed and manufacturing interests. It was the split between the owners of the coal-mines and cotton mills, whose sole concern was to produce as much as possible as cheaply as possible and as quickly as possible, and their employees whose interest lay in getting a share of the proceeds in their wage packets large enough to keep them alive and make their working and living conditions tolerable. In a time of unemployment, of no labour organization and no legal pro-tection against exploitation and industrial inhumanity, the wage-earners were helplessly exposed to every kind of abuse. Workers under the old domestic system, such as the surviv-ing handloom weavers, suffered new rigours because they could not compete with the new factories. Workers in the new factories were little better off. When women could be employed in coal-mines, small children in cotton mills, and all for twelve or fourteen hours a day, no bargaining about wages was possible. Each had to take what work he could get, there was no hope of returning to the land when so many farms were being deserted and so many labourers unemployed, and employers were able, by ingenious methods of payment in kind and fining for trivial offences, to mulct the worker of even his meagre wages. Of the nefarious device of the 'tommy-shop', where workers were forced to buy from their employer goods on account of their wages, Benjamin Disraeli wrote like this:

> The door of Mr Diggs' tommy-shop opened. The rush was like the advance into the pit of a theatre when the drama existed; pushing, squeezing, fighting, tearing, shrieking. On a high seat, guarded by rails from all contact, sat Mr Diggs, senior, with a bland smile on his sanctified countenance, a pen behind his ear, and recommending his constrained customers in honeyed tones to be patient and orderly. Behind the substantial counter, which was an impregnable fortification, was his popular son, Master Joseph; a short, ill-favoured cur with a spirit of vulgar oppression and malicious mischief stamped on his visage. His black, greasy lank hair, his pug nose, his coarse red face, and his projecting tusks, contrasted with the mild and lengthened countenance of his father, who looked very much like a wolf in sheep's clothing.
>
> For the first five minutes Master Joseph did nothing but blaspheme and swear at his customers, occasionally leaning over the counter and cuffing the women in the van or lugging some girl by the hair ...
>
> 'Don't make a brawling here,' said Master Joseph, 'or I'll jump over this here counter and knock you down, like nothink. What did you say, woman? are you deaf? what did you say? how much best tea do you want?'
>
> 'I don't want any, sir.'
>
> 'You never want best tea; you must take three ounces of best tea, or you shan't have nothing. If you say another word, I'll put you down four. You tall gal, what's your name, you keep back there, or I'll fetch you such a cut as'll keep you at home till next reckoning ...

Cuss them; I'll keep them quiet': and so he took up a yard measure, and, leaning over the counter hit right and left.

'Oh! you little monster!' exclaimed a woman, 'you have put out my baby's eye.'

There was a murmur; almost a groan. 'Whose baby's hurt?' asked Master Joseph, in a softened tone.

'Mine, sir,' said an indignant voice; 'Mary Church.'

'Oh! Mary Church, is it!' said the malicious imp; 'then I'll put Mary Church down for half a pound of best arrowroot; that's the finest thing in the world for babbies, and will cure you of bringing your cussed monkeys here, as if you all thought our shop was a hinfant school.'

Disraeli published this novel, *Sybil*, in 1845. He gave it the sub-title of *The Two Nations*, and thought it necessary to warn his readers in a foreword that the author had not been 'tempted to some exaggeration in the scenes that he has drawn', but that 'the descriptions, generally, are written from his own observation'. *Sybil* ends with the advance of an outraged mob on Diggs' tommy-shop, which they burned to the ground; such were the symbols of petty oppression which provoked riots and strikes in early Victorian England.

Lancashire, the home of the cotton industry, saw many such battles in the class-war between Disraeli's 'two nations'. The wonder is that the war never became open revolution. In the summer of 1819 a large crowd of some 60,000 people assembled in St Peter's Fields in Manchester, chiefly to hear the famous radical orator Hunt. When the mounted yeomanry were sent by the magistrates to arrest Hunt they charged the crowd, killed eleven people and wounded some four hundred, including over a hundred women. The 'massacre of Peterloo' passed into popular mythology and did much to offset the Tory credit for Waterloo. The younger Whigs like Macaulay, even the mill-owners themselves and the middle classes generally, were made more aware of the dangers of mere repression.

The Times, four days after Peterloo, pointed the moral which the more liberal sections of middle-class opinion drew from it:

> The more attentively we have considered the relations subsisting between the upper and the labouring classes throughout some of the manufacturing districts, the more painful and unfavourable is the construction which we are forced to put upon the events of last Monday . . . The two great divisions of society there, are – the masters, who have reduced the rate of wages; and the workmen, who complain of their masters for having done so. Turn the subject as we please, 'to this complexion it must come at last'.

The first reaction of the Government was repression, and the famous Six Acts were passed in the winter after Peterloo. They were intended to prevent large public meetings, kill or at least control severely the radical press, and undermine the whole movement for radical reforms. For a time they succeeded. But repeatedly throughout the century reforms were effected only as concessions to extreme pressure from below, and as alternatives to riot.

When it came to the question of public order, the landed gentry were even more ferocious in suppressing discontent than the mill-owners would have been, as the story of Peterloo illustrates. Until the successful installation of Sir Robert Peel's police force – which began in the metropolis in 1829 but did not extend to the whole country until the middle of the century – the machinery for keeping order was very defective. When put into action it had all the ferocity of nervous inefficiency. In *Eothen,* which Alexander Kinglake (1809–91) published in 1844, the author satirized the attitude of the English upper classes to the problems of both industrialism and public order. He is describing an interview between an English traveller and a Turkish Pasha, conducted by the intermediary of a Dragoman.

> *Dragoman:* No, your excellency, but he says the English talk by wheels and by steam.

Traveller: That's an exaggeration; but say that the English really have carried machinery to great perfection. Tell the Pasha (he'll be struck with that) that whenever we have any disturbances to put down, even at two or three hundred miles from London, we can send troops by the thousand to the scene of action in a few hours.

Dragoman (recovering his temper and freedom of speech): His Excellency, this Lord of Mudcombe, observes to your Highness, that whenever the Irish, or the French, or the Indians rebel against the English, whole armies of soldiers and brigades of artillery are dropped into a mighty chasm called Euston Square, and, in the biting of a cartridge, they rise up again in Manchester, or Dublin, or Paris, or Delhi, and utterly exterminate the enemies of England from the face of the earth.

Pasha: I know it – I know all: the particulars have been faithfully related to me, and my mind comprehends locomotives. The armies of the English ride upon the vapours of boiling caldrons, and their horses are flaming coals! – whirr! whirr! all by wheels! – whiz! whiz! all by steam ... The ships of the English swarm like flies; their printed calicoes cover the whole earth, and by the side of their swords the blades of Damascus are blades of grass. All India is but an item in the ledger-books of the merchants, whose lumber-rooms are filled with ancient thrones! – whirr! whirr! all by wheels! – whiz! whiz! all by steam!

Dragoman: The Pasha compliments the cutlery of England, and also the East India Company.

Traveller: The Pasha's right about the cutlery ... but I should like him to know, though, that we have got something in England besides that. These foreigners are always fancying that we have nothing but ships and railways, and East India Companies; do just tell the Pasha that our rural districts deserve his attention, and that even within the last two hundred years there has been an evident improvement in the culture of the turnip ...

The period 1830–50 was the era of railways and steam-ships in Britain. The background noises to all the seething movements of reform were not only the whirring and clatter of the cotton-mills, but the clanging of permanent ways and the hissing of the new locomotives. When the Duke of Wellington attended the opening of the new Manchester and Liverpool Railway in September 1830, he witnessed an event as important in its own way as the Battle of Waterloo which he had won fifteen years before. It symbolized the conquest of space and of parochialism. 'Parliamentary Reform must follow soon after the opening of this road,' wrote a Manchester man of the time: 'A million of persons will pass over it in the course of this year, and see that hitherto unseen village of Newton; and they must be convinced of the absurdity of its sending two members to Parliament, whilst Manchester sends none.' Between 1825 and 1835 fifty-four Railway Acts of all kinds went through Parliament. During the two years 1836–7 thirty-nine more bills for new lines in Great Britain were passed, and these were the boom years of railway construction, which added over 1000 miles to the railroads of the country. A second big boom came in the years 1844–7, and by 1848 some 5000 miles of railways were working in the United Kingdom, of which less than 400 were in Ireland. Fierce resistance came from the canal companies and from the turnpike trusts and coaching interests that ran the roads. Here again was a big conflict of interests, but everywhere the railroads won. The demand for coal and iron which this vast construction caused stimulated the development of the heavy industries, encouraged the rise of big contractors, and offered employment to thousands ranging from the gangs of navvies who laid the tracks to the drivers, firemen, and other staffs which ran the lines. A great new industry was born in little more than twenty years.

'At once cause and effect,' writes Professor J. H. Clapham, 'railway development coincided with a development of metallurgy and mining quite without precedent.' In 1815 Britain's output of iron was little more than a quarter of a million tons a year; by 1835 it was 1 million and by 1848 2 million tons. Coal output increased in proportion: from some 16 million tons in 1815 to 30 million by 1835 and 50 million by 1848. But engineering proper, and the industries devoted to making machines, were still small-scale. The main progress in engineering technique came only after 1848, and with it the rise of a big engineering and machine-tool industry. This was the process which turned the average Englishman from a countryman into an urban industrial worker, and thereby marks off the century since 1850 as a new era in the whole of English history.

The spread of social distress and economic upheaval, combined with the various conflicts of economic interest just described, created what soon came to be called 'the condition of England question'. To this 'question' various men and various movements gave very varied answers. Some of these answers are highly revealing as to how Englishmen thought and felt at the time, and are extremely important for subsequent developments in English politics and social thought. Broadly speaking, they fall into two categories: the highly personal and somewhat paternal answers of certain sensitive individuals, such as Robert Owen (1771–1858), Lord Shaftesbury (1801–85), and John Stuart Mill (1806–73): and early efforts at self-help on the part of the depressed classes, led by men of the lower-middle or artisan classes, such as Francis Place (1771–1854), William Lovett (1800–77), and a large number of lesser figures. The social history of this period can be understood largely through the lives and achievements of these men. But behind the reflections of the new social thinkers, the experiments of the philanthropists, and the successes of the popular leaders, there was fermenting a new spirit of discontent. Life in the new industrial towns, the discipline of the factories and the strenuous, incessant activity of the mines and mills in which men were harnessed to machines, all meant great problems of human adjustment. Country-bred men live by custom, and in the new environment custom was killed and habit shaken. 'In such an age,' as Dr and Mrs Hammond put it, 'the inequalities of life are apt to look less like calamities from the hand of heaven and more like injustices from the hand of man.' Unrest bred in such surroundings would seek social expression, political means of improvement, and would be turned against the most visible symbols of oppression. It seems likely to be true, as many historians have contended, that the English working classes of the industrial revolution were relatively better off than their ancestors: that degree of material improvement served – as with the French peasants of the days before 1789 – only to increase and broaden their discontent. The essence of the 'condition of England question' was that Englishmen were at last seeking, primitively and impatiently, for the reason why their condition was not better still.

The Philanthropists

To this central question Robert Owen, who came of lower middle-class parentage, provided a simple and coherent answer: that the condition of Englishmen would improve only when they replaced competition by cooperation as the mainspring of their social life and their economic activities. It is in this sense that he is correctly called the father of English socialism. He proclaimed that a social question demanded a social answer. If social conditions are bad – change them: in so far as they are bad because men are bad and behave inhumanely to their fellow-men, let men undergo a change of heart. He was a moralist as much as he was a socialist. He was, in every sense, a self-made man. Born and brought up as a shopkeeper, he was a man whose career most strongly appealed to a nation of shopkeepers. At the age of nineteen he became a manager in one of the cotton mills of Manchester, and seven years later he bought for himself and his partners the mills at New Lanark. In 1800 he began his great experiment designed to show that it actually paid an employer to treat his workers well. Taking over a concern which had lived on child labour drafted from Edinburgh and Glasgow and was staffed largely by thieves and drunkards, he turned it within a few years into a model business, which many men of power and wealth went on pilgrimage to visit. Every aspect of modern welfare-work was undertaken, ranging from public health, temperance, and education to provision of social security. All this he achieved while also making an adequate and even handsome profit for the mill-owners: and that was what most impressed his contemporaries. He achieved it by the force of his personality, and devoted the rest of his life to trying to develop the experiment in the direction of self-help and self-government. A voluntary and freely self-governing co-operative community was his ideal – such as he tried to find in his model colony 'New Harmony' in Indiana. This he never achieved, and New Harmony was a decisive, if not an entirely dismal, failure. Like many other self-made, successful, and spectacularly prosperous business men he became more and more a dreamer of dreams. Unlike the Carnegies and the Rockefellers, he had the courage of his convictions enough to sink his whole being and his whole fortune in these utopian experiments. He spent both in the service of causes which were far less influential or successful than that in which he had made his fame and his fortune. Socialistic communities repelled most of the men who mattered in the first half of the nineteenth century: but the damning, perplexing example of New Lanark could never be completely explained away, long after New Harmony was dead and forgotten. It might actually *pay* to be a good employer: did that mean that you might be losing if you were a bad one?

If even philanthropy could make profits then the men of Manchester were interested in philanthropy.

Completely a crank, something of a prig, but very much of a saint, the Welshman who brought enlightenment to Scotland left a profound impression on Englishmen. His super-abundant writings penetrated to people who were less likely to be won over by his record of practical success. He founded a tradition and almost a school of socialistic thought which runs down to the Fabian Society, the Cooperative movement, and beyond both into the present British Labour Party itself. The basis of nearly all his thoughts was the belief in a sort of material determinism: our characters are made for us by environment and heredity alike, and therefore we are not at all responsible for what we are:

> Every day will make it more and more evident that the character of man is, without a single exception, always formed for him; that it may be, and is, chiefly, created by his predecessors; that they give him, or may give him, his ideas and habits, which are the powers that govern and direct his conduct. Man, therefore, never did, nor is it possible he ever can, form his own character. (*A New View of Society, Third Essay.*)

This being so, education is the panacea for all ills. Men can all recognize truth when it is placed before them, and by moulding men's minds to the truth, society and even human nature can be revolutionized. Here was a simple and powerful basis for any programme of comprehensive reform. Practised with zest in his early days, and preached incessantly with boundless enthusiasm in his latter days, these simple notions spread wide and sank deep as one possible answer to the problems of social distress which could no longer be cheerfully ignored.

Very different in origins and in character, though also something of a saint, was Antony Ashley Cooper, eldest son of the sixth Earl of Shaftesbury. His life also was given, with

single-minded religious zeal, to the cause of social philanthropy, and he is the father of all nineteenth-century
factory legislation. His answer to the 'condition of England
question' was more political than Owen's; it was that the
State, through legislation and systematic regulation, should
control conditions in factories, the length of the working day,
and similar sources of inhumanity and distress. Even more
paternal and patriarchal in outlook than Owen, he taught
the governing classes of England to assume some responsibility for the welfare of the people. His first parliamentary
victory was the Factory Act of 1833. All Factory Acts,
except the original Act of 1802 which was promoted by Sir
Robert Peel the elder, and which limited child labour to
twelve hours a day without night work, had applied to
paupers in cotton mills. The Act of 1833 still affected only
children but it applied to nearly all textile mills. After 1833
no child under eleven for the first year, under twelve for the
second, and under thirteen for the third, was to be employed
for more than forty-eight hours a week, or more than nine
in one day. No person under eighteen was to be employed
more than sixty-nine hours a week, or more than twelve
hours in one day. Of these periods, an hour and a half each
day was to be allowed for meals, and children of the protected age-groups were to attend school for at least two
hours each day. Above all the Act provided for inspection.
Four full-time inspectors were appointed, with wide powers,
so that the new regulations had 'teeth' in them. It was
passed by Parliament partly to steal the thunder of the
demands, of Ashley and others, for a Ten-Hour Bill limiting
the working hours of adults: in this it succeeded, for the
Ten-Hours Bill, limiting the daily working hours of women
and young people, did not pass until 1847.

In their admirable biography of Lord Shaftesbury, Dr and
Mrs Hammond have described his subsequent collabora-

tion with Edwin Chadwick and other Radical reformers over the improvement of public health, his work on behalf of the agricultural labourers, starting with those on his father's scandalously run estates which he inherited in 1851, his support for reform of the lunacy laws, and his efforts to better the lot of boy chimney-sweeps. All such humanitarian causes enlisted his backing, and seldom is a public career so single-minded and so consistent in its purpose as was Shaftesbury's. So stiff was his character that aristocratic benevolence was never replaced in his make-up by a spirit of comradeship or a readiness to cooperate in movements for working-class self-help. He ended his days a lonely and somewhat isolated figure, clinging to his aristocratic principles of *noblesse oblige*, wrapt in his own religious conscience, and distrusting the new spirit of mass-organization and democratic politics to the growth of which he had almost unwittingly contributed.

If the career of Owen illustrates a middle-class response, and that of Shaftesbury an aristocratic response, to the challenge of their time, the life and thought of John Stuart Mill exemplify the intellectual and theoretical adjustments which had to be made in the prevailing creed of Radicalism by honest men who sought a new creed more appropriate to the changing social scene. His *Autobiography* is one of the most revealing and attractive documents of the time. Educated by his father, James Mill, in the most orthodox principles of the Benthamite philosophy of utilitarianism, he found himself forced by its inherent crudity and its inadequacies for the rapidly changing conditions of his lifetime to re-state it as a creed of democratic radicalism. In doing this he found himself imperceptibly becoming a Socialist. His famous essay *On Liberty* is a classic of democratic theory because it shows how an honest and sensitive mind grappled with these problems.

He describes how, from the age of fifteen when he first read Bentham, he had one object in life: 'to be a reformer of the world'. He was that peculiar product of the nineteenth century, a professional reformer; prepared to make reform an almost full-time occupation, a career, even a crusade. By dint of the agony of his own spiritual experience when he came to abandon the rigid creed of his father, he perceived the fallacy in Benthamism: its debased conception of human happiness as a mere arithmetical sum of physical pleasures. He learnt that happiness is a state of mind and being, a condition of spirit, and not the total result of merely seeking pleasure and avoiding pain. This discovery led him to revolutionize Benthamism, for the distinction between higher and lower pleasures undermined the whole basis of the materialist philosophy of utilitarianism: 'better Socrates dissatisfied', as he put it, 'than a fool satisfied'. His honest good sense rebelled against the notion that push-pin is as 'good' as poetry if it gives the same 'amount' of pleasure. From this fundamental change much else followed. It followed, for example, that human liberty means more than just leaving the individual alone to pursue his own selfish pleasures, and is a social pursuit of 'the greatest happiness of the greatest number' by deliberate and possibly coercive measures. It followed, too, that legislation must have a more positive function in society than Bentham had allowed: it must seek to enable men to exercise their natural capacities, use their talents, and develop their personalities, untrammelled by artificial legal impediments and evil economic conditions. The good society, for Mills, is one of the richest diversity derived from the free interplay of human character and personality; he saw that to attain anything like that society in nineteenth-century Britain a long series of far-reaching reforms would be necessary. These reforms would mean a breach with the crude doctrines of *laissez-faire*, a profound modification of the notion of a 'natural harmony of interests' whereby each pursuing his own good (i.e. his own profit in business and his own pleasure in social life) would automatically promote the general good.

He championed the cause of popular education, of trade-union organization, of the cooperative movement, of the emancipation of women. He could rejoice that 'the poor have now come out of their leading strings, and cannot any longer be governed or treated like children'. He broke sharply, in his teaching, with the paternalism of Owen and Shaftesbury and even of Bentham. Self-government was better than 'good' government imposed by authority, because it allowed men and women to be educated by experience and by responsibility. Progress, he believed, came from mental energy and spiritual enterprise, and truth emerged from the free interplay of educated and well-developed minds. He had faith in the governing influence of ideas and ideals: 'one person with a belief is a social power equal to ninety-nine who have only interests'. He was, in the fullest sense of that much abused but fine word, a democrat.

Was Mill a Socialist? In his *Autobiography* he called himself one. But it was a pragmatic and un-doctrinaire socialism that he believed in. He defined the great end of social improvement as being 'to fit mankind by cultivation for a state of society combining the greatest personal freedom with that just distribution of the fruits of labour, which the present laws of property do not profess to aim at'. Whether private property or communal ownership would best serve this end he regarded as 'a question which must be left, as it safely may', to the people of a later generation to decide. We, of that later generation, are still confronted with that choice. He looked forward to a time when 'the rule that they who do not work shall not eat will be applied not only to paupers only but impartially to all'. Yet he was certainly nothing of a Marxist. While he wrote Karl Marx was also living in London, working at the British Museum on his great work on *Capital* and vigorously engaged in the intricate politics of the International. Mill never mentions, and does not even seem to have heard of, Karl Marx. His Socialism was of a purely English and indigenous stock, although he sharpened his ideas on his knowledge of the French socialist writers of the 1830 and 1848 revolutions. Mill is the most complete example of how English democratic traditions, dating from the time of John Locke and the English Revolution of 1688, and comprising by this period the radicalism of the eighteenth century and the utilitarianism of the nineteenth, adjusted themselves to the challenge of a new industrial age. They have gone on developing along these same lines ever since.

The Artisan Reformers

Meanwhile, thanks to the activities of men like Francis Place and William Lovett, the artisan and labouring classes were gaining both the legal right and the social experience of free association and self-help. Vast tasks of popular education and enlightenment were called for. The 'mob' of the early industrial revolution was an anti-Jacobin, anti-Papal, anti-Dissenter force. It laughed at the French and Bonaparte, it rioted against Popery under the leadership of Lord George Gordon, it burned down the houses and meeting-places of Protestant Dissenters like Dr Joseph Priestley. It was hostile to Radicalism. But after 1815 this mood changed. Social grievances and political abuses turned popular attention towards the cause of domestic reform, and in this mood the Combination Laws of the time around 1800 came to be bitterly resented. These laws, passed during the French wars, made working-class organization illegal and laid trade unions open to new charges of 'conspiracy'. Manufacturers came to support the repeal of these laws, on the ground that they caused rather than prevented trouble, and sought in return the support of the workers for their own causes of free trade and parliamentary reform. In these conditions Francis Place, the famous 'Radical tailor of Charing Cross', was able to press for the repeal of the Combination Acts. He and most of his middle-class supporters did not want repeal to make trade-union organization easier; they believed that once workers had the legal right to free association and collective bargaining with their employers it would be unnecessary for them to use the right, and trade unions would die a natural death. It was the logical application of the principles of *laissez-faire:* a free field for all and no favour would promote the general good. Presenting the case for repeal in these terms, Place and his chief agent in Parliament, the private member Joseph Hume, with consummate skill steered their bill through Parliament in 1824. The bill settled the status of trade unions in terms of equality with employers' associations. It was followed by an epidemic of strikes, Peel and Huskisson wanted to reverse the policy, and in 1825 a second Act was passed severely restricting intimidation and the use of violence. Had it been rigidly enforced trade unions might even now have found their activities immensely hampered and very dangerous to those who led them. But absolute prohibition had gone, the governments were no longer in a mood for savage repression, and in fact the trade unions so extensively used their limited rights that the decade between 1825 and 1835 saw a remarkable growth in trade unions. The disguise of Friendly Societies, which had often been used to mask trade union organizations, was no longer needed and they could come out into the open. New unions were formed, with open constitutions and published books of rules. Bargains about conditions of work, wages, and apprenticeship were freely made, though as events were to show running such bodies could still be a dangerous occupation.

Naturally enough, the early attempts at big-scale organization were too ambitious and too vague for the conditions of the time to justify. The most ambitious venture of all was Robert Owen's famous Grand National Consolidated Trades Union which claimed over half a million members. It proved to be neither very grand, nor national, nor consolidated: indeed it was scarcely, in the modern sense, a trade union. Under its inspiration or example countless schemes for the complete reorganization of economic life on cooperative lines were put forward: a proposed 'Grand National Union of Builders' would take over and run the entire building trade of the country, and so on. Through his 'equitable labour exchanges' and the use of 'labour notes' as currency, Owen proposed to build a new labour commonwealth. It was all very utopian, given the state of development both of working-class education and self-consciousness, and the condition of British industry itself at that time. By 1834 the project collapsed, not in one vast general strike which might open a new day, but in many local, sporadic, and usually futile strikes and lock-outs. The death-blow was delivered by the government and judiciary in the shape of the famous Tolpuddle prosecution.

A handful of Dorchester agricultural labourers, headed by George Loveless, formed a union which was to be part of the Grand National Consolidated. Because they adopted initiation oaths and ceremonies they were prosecuted for administering 'unlawful oaths'. The men were tried and sentenced to transportation for seven years. *The Times* of 1834 reported it like this:

> *John Lock:* . . . We all went into Thomas Stanfield's house into a room upstairs. John Stanfield came to the door of the room. I saw

James Lovelace and George Lovelace go along the passage. One of the men asked if we were ready. We said, yes. One of them said, 'Then bind your eyes', and we took out handkerchiefs and bound over our eyes. They then led us to another room on the same floor. Someone then read a paper, but I don't know what the meaning of it was. After that we were asked to kneel down, which we did. Then there was some more reading: I don't know what it was about. It seemed to be out of some part of the Bible. Then we got up and took the bandages off our eyes. I had then seen James Lovelace and John Stanfield in the room. Some one read again, but I don't know what it was, and then we were told to kiss the book, which looked like a little Bible. I then saw all the prisoners there. James Lovelace had on a white dress, it was not a smock-frock. They told us the rules, that we should have to pay 1s. then, and 1d. a week afterwards, to support the men when they were standing out from their work. They said we were as brothers; that when we were to stop for wages we should not tell our masters ourselves, but that the masters would have a note or a letter sent to them.

The rules of the little society included (No. 23) the statement:

> That the object of this society can never be promoted by any act or acts of violence, but, on the contrary, all such proceedings must tend to injure the cause and destroy the society itself. This order therefore will not countenance any violation of the laws.

In 1836 the remainder of their sentence was remitted, but the case of the 'Tolpuddle Martyrs' became a landmark in trade-union history. Owen and his friends abolished all such ceremonies of initiation and planned a great series of protests against the sentences. Owen liquidated his Grand National Union and abandoned the cause of unionism for that of cooperative movements. Many of the component parts of it survived and contented themselves with more modest efforts to ensure collective bargaining in industry, without attempting a general challenge to the whole economic system. On this basis the modern unions grew and gained in strength, forming a solid foundation for the further rapid growth of labour organization after 1850. Owen and

Place had launched a movement more powerful than either could foresee when he died: and much more powerful than Place and his Radical colleagues would ever have desired.

In these ways the first twenty years after Waterloo saw a wide diversity of responses to the new conditions of post-war England. On the part of the Tory and Liberal-Tory governments, the chief reply to social unrest was repression, but already signs of a readiness for graceful withdrawal were evident. The middle classes, divided between the frightened landed gentry and mill-owners and the more liberal-minded and philanthropical sections, were torn between policies of repression and concession. The workers, still finding leadership from above rather than from among themselves, were groping their way towards self-help, trade-union and cooperative organization, and the claim to legal protection for their activities. For another twenty years they sought remedy for their economic distress mainly in political reforms. In 1836 William Lovett, a cabinet-maker, founded the London Working Men's Association of respectable and self-educated artisans, and two years later he and Francis Place drew up and published the 'People's Charter' as the political programme of their society. Its essential demands were for a more thorough-going overhaul of the electoral and parliamentary system as it was left by the Whig Reform Bill of 1832. Before considering the meaning of Chartism, it is necessary to examine the series of important constitutional and political reforms carried out by the Whig-Liberal governments of the 1830s. These reforms, by disrupting the old social and political compromise which had lasted throughout most of the eighteenth century, prepared the way for a great new transformation of both the British system of government and British social policy.

CHAPTER III

CONSTITUTIONAL AND POLITICAL REFORMS

The New Social Balance

THE great political and constitutional settlement of 1688 had survived in substance all through the eighteenth century because it represented a remarkably solid and comprehensive compromise between various sections of the population. The landed gentry had votes as 40s. freeholders in the counties and often held great power as the local magistrates: a goodly proportion of their number sat in the House of Commons, and their sons had access to trade, politics, or the professions as they chose. The big landowners enjoyed great wealth from their extensive estates, the agricultural prosperity of the enclosures, and the general stability of the national economy. They dominated the House of Lords and the councils of the king, controlled foreign policy, served as lords-lieutenant of the counties in charge of the local militia, and nominated large retinues of relations and dependents to places in the Commons, the Church, the Army, and indeed all public services. The merchant and business classes, ranging from the financiers who were fund-holders of the national debt guaranteed through the Bank of England and the nabobs of the East India Company down to the smaller traders, manufacturers, and shopkeepers, enjoyed great freedom of enterprise and plentiful opportunities for that enterprise within the colonial empire bequeathed to England by Lord Chatham after the Seven Years' War (1756–63). The professional classes – literary giants like

Edward Gibbon, painters like Sir Joshua Reynolds and Gainsborough, master craftsmen like Chippendale and Wedgwood – throve on the patronage of the wealthy aristocrats and merchants. They also enjoyed a ready and appreciative middle-class public of gentry and townsfolk. The 'masses' counted for little in politics and as yet felt little conflict of interest with the 'classes'. Eighteenth-century England was a close-knit, organic social unity. The stable political and constitutional system of that period reflected this deep and solid social equilibrium.

Into this community came the disturbing and disruptive forces of industrialism and radicalism. The great wars of the French Revolutionary and Napoleonic era for a time altered the flow of these forces. Industrialization, temporarily diverted into war-industries, proceeded apace after the wars. Radicalism, with its demands for a complete overhaul of the parliamentary system, was pent-up during the wars and then subjected to the period of repression after the wars which has already been described. The new social balance and the new political doctrines in combination made some overhaul of the political system inevitable. It was all a question of how much and how far it should be readjusted to fit the new shape of English life and ideas.

The essence of the movements for parliamentary reform in the first generation of the nineteenth century was the claim of new forms of wealth – manufacturing and commercial – to assert their place alongside landed property as the basis of social prestige and political power. The Whig spokesmen of these mercantile and industrial interests were in most cases content that property and not people should still be regarded as what parliament ought to represent: but they wanted such changes as would admit the industrialists and merchants to representation in parliament. The Radicals, heirs of the Wilkesites, Tom Paine, and the American and French Revolutionaries, wanted persons and not property to be the subject of representation. One man one vote, universal suffrage, was their first demand. The movements for political reforms were split between these two main schools of thought. The Whigs got their way in 1832, in the first Reform Bill: the Radicals, after a century of intermittent but very persistent agitation, got their way only in 1928, when full universal suffrage was achieved. Before even the first Reform Bill could be passed, the privileges of the eighteenth-century landed gentry in ecclesiastical matters were attacked, and after it their powers in local government were likewise weakened. In this sense, the whole series of political and constitutional reforms in the decade between 1828 and 1838 was one composite attack on the legal privileges of the landed interest which the shift of wealth, power, and population to the towns and factories and ports had already rendered out of date and anomalous. It is important for understanding Victorian England that these piecemeal reforms should be seen as one whole process, making in one direction; and also that these political and constitutional reforms should be seen in their close relationship to the economic reforms which accompanied and succeeded them. To this task this and the following chapter are devoted.

The Fight for Religious Equality

For Roman Catholics and most kinds of Protestant dissenters the legacy of the eighteenth century was a set of legal disabilities. The Toleration Act of 1689 had given the latter some protection for freedom of religious worship, but the former none. The tolerant temper of the eighteenth century, combined with the proven worth of Protestant dissenters as reliable British citizens, had won them considerable toleration in practice, and had even opened the doors of civil and military office to all whose consciences would stretch a little. In the main they were still formally excluded from ministerial or administrative office, from commissions in the armed services, and from the universities: and Roman Catholics, in addition to all these disabilities, were subject to occasional persecution even for practising their religion. The town mobs, fiercely Anglican in the first half of the eighteenth century until they became equally ferociously Radical and Wilkesite in the second half, could as late as 1780 be roused to persecuting violence by a madman like Lord George Gordon. In 1807 Sydney Smith, in the *Letters of Peter Plymley*, remarked:

> When a country squire hears of an ape, his first feeling is to give it nuts and apples; when he hears of a Dissenter his immediate impulse is to commit it to the County Jail, to shave its head, to alter its customary food, and to have it privately whipped.

Although, as he points out, there were even then some forty-five Dissenters in one House of Parliament, and sixteen in the other, sitting for Scotland, there were no Catholic members of the Commons. Both in formal enactment and in popular prejudice Papists were still, after Waterloo, regarded as too dangerously disloyal to be admitted to any post of power or responsibility.

Agitation for removal of these old discriminations against British citizens on religious grounds grew during the war. In 1810 a Protestant Society for the Protection of Religious Liberty was formed by the Protestant dissenters, with the aim of getting the Test and Corporation Acts of Charles II repealed. Within the next ten years it won the support of Whigs like Lord John Russell and Lord Holland, and in 1812 and 1813 piecemeal measures eased the legal position of the dissenters. The growing numbers and strength of Methodism greatly reinforced the demand for some relaxation of the Anglican monopoly of office in the State: non-conformists by now numbered some two million out of a population of thirteen million. When Russell moved a resolution to consider the repeal of the Test and Corporation Acts he pointed out the evil results of 'mixing politics with religion', and secured a Commons majority of forty-four. His subsequent Bill was opposed by Peel and Palmerston, but met with little solid opposition in either House and became law in 1828. The old ideal of 'one State – one Church' had been renounced, and the principle of religious equality made its first great step forward. Meanwhile the corresponding issue of Roman Catholic emancipation had also raised its head: and that, since it aroused even deeper prejudices, was more difficult.

In 1800 George III refused to violate his coronation oath by 'putting Papists and Presbyterians in a state of equality with the Church of England', and Pitt's wise attempt to conciliate Ireland by timely concession was frustrated.

Sydney Smith, Canon of St Paul's and a very famous wit, took up the cause of Catholic emancipation in his powerful *Letters of Peter Plymley*, already mentioned. He expressed pithily and trenchantly the attitude of the tolerant Anglican, pleading the cause both on grounds of national security and necessity, as the basis for national unity and for settlement in Ireland in face of the Napoleonic menace, and on grounds of common sense.

> You say the King's coronation oath will not allow him to consent to any relaxation of the Catholic laws. – Why not relax the Catholic laws as well as the laws against Protestant dissenters? If one is contrary to his oath, the other must be so too; for the spirit of the oath is, to defend the Church establishment, which the Quaker and the Presbyterian differ from as much or more than the Catholic . . . Nothing would give me such an idea of security, as to see twenty or thirty Catholic gentlemen in Parliament, looked upon by all the Catholics as the fair and proper organ of their party.

The truth was that discrimination against Catholics had become an anachronism on both political and ecclesiastical grounds, and the writings of the famous and popular Anglican writer exposed the inconsistencies and absurdities of the position in the most devastating way. They deserve study by all who want to understand the religious issues of early nineteenth-century England.[1]

It was in Ireland that the issue was most burning. Catholics in England numbered only some 60,000 and were quiet and loyal. In Ireland the disabilities kept the great majority of the population from holding political office and were the first bulwark of the political ascendancy of the Protestant English interest in Ireland. Daniel O'Connell (1775–1847) 'the Liberator', revived an older Catholic Association, based on a wide popular membership with the famous penny-a-month subscription or 'Catholic rent'. Its aim was to promote the candidature of Protestant Members of Parliament pledged to support Catholic emancipation at Westminster: but even this eminently constitutional procedure did not prevent the suppression of the association in 1829. The issue haunted English politics throughout the ministries of Liverpool, Canning, and Goderich, and divided the ministry headed by the Duke of Wellington which, in 1829, eventually passed the Roman Catholic Relief Act. When O'Connell was returned by the voters of County Clare, despite his legal incapacity to sit, the danger arose that if every Catholic constituency followed suit deadlock and civil war would be the result. As so often in nineteenth-century England, the threat of disorder alone generated the steam to blow through a fundamental reform. Sir Robert Peel, the Duke's Home Secretary and a traditional opponent of Catholic emancipation, was converted to it in face of this danger, as he was converted two decades later to the repeal of the Corn Laws

1. A modern edition was published in 1929, edited by G. C. Heseltine.

by famine in Ireland. He helped to put through the bill. So it was that the 'Victor of Waterloo' came to 'let the Papists into Parliament'. Roman Catholics were placed on the same civic footing as Protestant Dissenters, and in England and Scotland all public official posts save a few (such as those of Monarch, Regent, and Lord Chancellor) were thrown open to any citizen of the United Kingdom whose capacity fitted him for them, regardless of his religious beliefs. To a large measure public life was separated from private religion, and citizenship from churchmanship. On this liberal basis a new social order and a new kind of State could be built.

In Ireland the result was less happy. Relief for Roman Catholics was accompanied by disfranchisement of the 40s. freeholders and the suppression of the Catholic Association. Religious equality was given with one hand, civil and political liberties were taken away with the other: a rankling sore remained to poison Anglo-Irish relations, and the political system of Ireland, until modern times.

In the United Kingdom universities were preserved as an Anglican monopoly for another generation. In 1854 and 1856 Dissenters of all creeds were at last admitted to Oxford and Cambridge, but were still debarred from the degree of Master of Arts, from all degrees in Divinity, and from all headships, professorships, and fellowships, and so from all share in the teaching, administration, and government of the universities. It was 1871 before the Universities Test Act became law, and it reserved a few posts for Anglicans only: six years later the present condition of equality in the Universities was substantially reached. The old ideal of uniformity and conformity took a long time to die, though it was doomed after 1829. There was still a State-Church: there was no longer a Church-State.

The Overhaul of Town Government

The new industrialism with the consequent growth of sprawling towns, combined with the aftermath of the wars, produced the twin evils of crime and poverty in much more acute forms. These put a great new strain upon the machinery of local government. In this period it was still as true as it had been in earlier centuries that most government was local government. The tasks of the central government were, primarily, the framing of national policy in foreign, commercial, and fiscal affairs, and the general maintenance and supervision of government internally. The day-to-day administration of the country was still conducted mainly on the periphery – in the localities themselves. It was in the hands of the corporations in the boroughs and the magistrates in the counties, where it had been for centuries. The rapid growth of population and the equally rapid redistribution of population over the face of Britain, the changing type of population produced by town life, the importunate evils of crime and poverty, made this old machinery out of date and hopelessly inadequate, most acutely in the towns.

The years between 1828 and 1835 saw a remarkable change of outlook and method in grappling with these problems. First in priority was the fundamental problem of public order. Our period opens with riots: the disturbances in London provoked by the new Corn Law of 1815. The crowds of rioters were unusually small for these times – never larger than fifty people – but authority was helpless in face of them. One such crowd attacked the house of Lord Chancellor Eldon in Bedford Square, broke its windows and tore up its railings, sacked its entrance hall and an adjoining room, and forced the Lord Chancellor to escape through the back premises into the grounds of the British Museum.

Eldon records that he 'brought into the house by their collars two of the mob, and told them that they would be hanged. One of them bid me look to myself, and told me that the people were much more likely to hang me than I was to procure any of them to be hanged.' These two culprits were in fact discharged by a magistrate because the soldiers present refused to serve as witnesses. Similar attacks were made on Mr Robinson who had introduced the Corn Law, on Lord Hardwicke, Lord Darnley, and others. Ministers regarded the occasional sacking of their houses as natural and inevitable, and yet were strangely reluctant to contemplate the creation of an efficient police force. The prevailing attitude to the questions of punishment and public order is well shown in the long struggle of men like Sir Samuel Romilly (1757–1818) to improve the penal code and of men like Sir Robert Peel (1788–1850) to secure the establishment of the modern police.

The normal reaction of Parliament to disorder was to increase the already excessively large number of offences for which the death penalty could be inflicted. In 1808 Romilly had announced in the House of Commons that he intended to devote himself to reform of the Criminal Code by diminishing the number of capital offences. This notion caused immediate alarm, but his bill for abolishing the death penalty for the crime of picking pockets of goods of the value of twelve pence (normally an offence of children) at last became law. Three more bills, which he brought in two years later, to remove further offences of theft from the list of capital crimes, were defeated: so were all his subsequent efforts save one – a bill abolishing hanging for stealing from a bleaching-ground cloth to the value of five shillings in England, or of ten shillings in Ireland. The main arguments brought against even these mild changes in the savage penal code were that national character and manners were moulded by the criminal law, that the removal of even one cog of the machine of punishment might bring disaster, and that the fear of death was essential to restrain the evil-doer. Typical of the whole chorus was the plea that 'the peace of the countryside would be cheaply purchased by the forfeiture of a few lives in order to deter future outrages on the property of individuals'. Plainly enough the policy of mere terror did not deter: for so long as detection and capture were so uncertain, and juries were reluctant to convict where conviction meant disproportionate penalties, these offences continued in abundance. Improved police methods were essential and were a logical part of any coherent programme of penal reform.

This connexion was little appreciated at that time. Romilly opposed the idea of improved police because he was critical of the existing methods of the Bow Street runners, the Thames police, and the watchmen and constables of the parishes. Reliance on the army as the ultimate protection against disorder, the normal eighteenth-century technique, had always proved both costly and unreliable. If the troops obeyed orders and fired, the result was civilian bloodshed and popular outcry: if they sympathized with the mob, as they did with Wilkes in 1769, the government was left helpless. In the Spa Fields riots of 1816, and again in the 'Peterloo Massacre' of 1817, military force proved a most inefficient weapon of order. The regular use of government spies and agents, to give preliminary warning of insurrections, was even more ineffective because of the character of the men employed. Like some of the Bow Street runners they were liable to accept payment from both sides with equanimity. The problem reached a climax in 1820 in the famous Cato Street Conspiracy. Arthur Thistlewood, one of the leaders of the Spa Fields riots and a fanatical and desperate idealist, was charged along with four other desperadoes with plotting to murder all the Ministers as the prelude to insurrection. It was a crazy plot, readily foiled and duly exaggerated by the government, for whom it was a godsend. But the sensation it caused gave some impetus to reform, and this impetus was greatly augmented in the same year by the threat of a mutiny among the 300 Guards on whom London's public order ultimately depended.

The first important convert to the need for police was no other than the Duke of Wellington. In a memorandum to the Prime Minister (Lord Liverpool) he wrote:

> In my opinion the Government ought, without the loss of a moment's time, to adopt measures to form either a police in London or military corps, which should be of a different description from the regular military force, or both.

Wellington had created a new police force in Ireland, which his successor Robert Peel had improved. These two men now took up the cause of police reform in England, and after nine years of pressure for it at last in 1829 carried it through Parliament. But they succeeded only in the face of constant opposition even from special Commissions created to examine the problem. That of 1822 included in its report a memorable judgement:

> It is difficult to reconcile an effective system of police with that perfect freedom of action and exemption from interference which are the great privileges and blessing of society in this country; and Your Committee think that the forfeiture or curtailment of such advantages are too great a sacrifice for improvements in police, or facilities in detection of crime, however desirable in themselves if abstractedly considered.

In that same year the champions of penal reform, now led by Sir James Mackintosh (1765–1832), Fowell Buxton (1786–1845), and William Wilberforce (1759–1833), joined hands with the champions of police reform, and the two movements became parts of one big campaign to improve public law and order, led by Peel who championed both causes. Its fruits were Peel's new Metropolitan Police Office at Scotland Yard, its force of 1000 men soon to be trebled, and the sound establishment of Britain's first effective civilian police under the charge of the Home Office. It was financed by a new 'police rate', levied on all within the Metropolitan area who paid the poor rate, so that crime and poverty were now openly associated, if only in the finance of the new organization, as interconnected social problems.

The new force, with its top hats and belted blue coats, was at first greeted with derision and hostility, much of which was connected with indignation against the new police rate. But gradually the police came to be accepted and respected. The security of the ordinary citizen was greatly increased and crime was checked. The force stood up well to the crisis of 1831, when it prevented in London a repetition of the Bristol riots. Within the following thirty years the example of the metropolis was imitated first by other towns and then by the counties. By establishing very early contact with disorder rather than waiting until it had grown too great to be quelled without bloodshed; by preventing mobs from forming rather than trying to disperse them after they had formed; by creating a spirit of civilian cooperation with the public in the common cause of good order; above all, by making the detection and punishment of offenders more inevitable and certain, Peel's police conferred an immense boon on the whole country. As London became too hot for the elements of crime and disorder they dispersed to other towns, and when these in turn adopted police methods the offenders moved on to the country districts. When the counties too adopted police forces, crime came to be increasingly held down. Partly in step with this movement, and partly as a consequence of it, moves for amendment of the Criminal Code also made headway.

Certainty of punishment rather than savagery of punishment became the ideal of public authorities: and both morals and manners, as well as civilization, improved.

The local authorities who in this way strengthened their hands against crime and disorder were also driven to tackle the problem of poverty. As already mentioned, the Speenhamland method of paying outdoor relief in aid of wages had developed and spread throughout large areas of the country after 1795. By 1830 its evil effects, both on the habits of the poor and the pockets of the ratepayers, were notorious. The difficulty was to find a way of cutting down the wasteful and demoralizing expenditure of public money without also causing excessive hardship to the deserving poor. The existing poor laws, some dating from the time of Queen Elizabeth, were a fearsome tangle of inconsistent and ineffective devices and regulations. Gilbert's Act of 1782 attempted to tidy up this tangle, but without great success. The principle of parochial responsibility, retained even by the Speenhamland methods, was no longer adequate. It meant that the burden of poor relief was spread very unevenly and unjustly, and led to the habit of taking villagers into the factories in good times but expelling them again to the villages in bad times, so as to save the burden of pauperism from falling on the towns. The administration of relief was wasteful and corrupt. By 1815, under the impetus given by Gilbert's Act, some 900 parishes had grouped themselves into sixty-seven 'Gilbert incorporations', or unions of blocks of parishes, to set up workhouses. As there were nearly 16,000 parishes in England and Wales, the whole matter was very confused. Existing workhouses were not just poorhouses – they organized spinning and weaving, but varied widely in efficiency and reputation. Those at Lincoln, Canterbury, Brighton, and Chichester were good, those at Oxford and Chatham were bad.

The drive for overhaul of the whole system came chiefly from Edwin Chadwick (1800–90), a disciple of Bentham. Under his encouragement and stimulus a Commission was set up and its famous Report of 1834 re-thought the whole problem and made a series of specific recommendations, most of which were then embodied in the Poor Law Amendment Act of that year. This procedure became the favourite and regular method of investigating social problems in Victorian England. The Commission concentrated mainly on the problem of how to deal with the able-bodied poor, and distinguished sharply between them and the aged, the sick, the orphan poor, and lunatics. All these categories had hitherto been handled indiscriminately in practice, although in principle Gilbert's Act, for example, had prescribed varying treatment for the various categories of poor. The Act of 1834 stipulated that outdoor relief be discontinued for the able-bodied and their families, except as regards medical relief and the apprenticeship of children. It provided for a transition period of two years, during which relief in kind was to be substituted for relief in money, and the whole administration of even relief in kind was to be greatly stiffened and restricted. It shifted responsibility from the parish vestries to new elected boards of Guardians, who were to work under the general direction and instruction of a new central authority, the Poor Law Commissioners. It therefore introduced several new principles into the whole administration of the country: more especially, elected local bodies and strong centralized control. Both devices were thereafter imitated for a whole series of social service organizations.

As regards relief of the poor, a basic principle of the Report of 1834 was national uniformity in the treatment of each separate class of paupers, but diversity of treatment for each class: so that the able-bodied should no longer be confused with the old and frail, or orphan children with lunatics, and the lot of the able-bodied should not vary merely according to the place in which they happened to live. This remained the official theory of the new law, but in practice the Commissioners did not fully enforce these principles. On the one hand the same workhouse was often used indiscriminately as poorhouse, orphanage, and asylum, and on the other some unions imposed harsher tests on the able-bodied than did others. These sound principles of the Report and the Act were often sacrificed to the quite different but in some respects more immediate purpose of abolishing extravagant outdoor relief. This principle, which the Act intended to be applied primarily to the able-bodied only, was too often applied to all poor persons indiscriminately, and the workhouse-test was used more harshly than was intended. Nevertheless, at the price of considerable human hardship in the short run, the reforms did succeed in checking the demoralization and pauperization of the working classes. The grouping of parishes into unions was greatly extended, so that by 1840 six-sevenths of the population lived in areas covered by poor-law unions, and by 1846 the 643 unions mostly had their own workhouses. The system of poor relief had certainly been improved. The old chaos had given place to a new pattern of public administration involving important new principles which could later be extended and adapted.

The effect on local government was considerable. The Justices of the Peace, the traditional 'maids-of-all-work' of local administration and the keystone of the local power of the landed gentry, had been deprived of a free hand in one of their most important of functions. The elected Guardians included the Justices *ex officio*, but now they had to share their responsibilities with elected members, and they had to submit to the directives of the three high-powered central

Commissioners at Somerset House. On the other hand, the parish vestries were still held separately responsible for meeting the costs of relieving their own poor, so there was centralization of control without centralization of financial responsibility. Imitation of this pattern was to lead, in the course of the century, to the conferring of new functions on a host of new, overlapping, and confusing local authorities other than the Justices of the Peace and the Borough Councils: until, by the last two decades of the century, the whole county administration also had to be completely overhauled and reconstructed. The Poor Law Commission lasted until 1847, when it was replaced by the Poor Law Board, under a minister responsible to Parliament: but its essential functions did not change until 1871, when it was merged into the new Local Government Board.

The workhouses created by this system loomed large in the life of the poor in mid nineteenth-century England, and life in them has been immortalized by the novels of Charles Dickens. Mr Bumble, the treatment of Oliver Twist, and the resentment of the honest working classes against the new tendency of petty officials to browbeat and tyrannize over them under the excuse of 'administering' them, gave great impetus to the growth of the first big movement of working-class self-help – Chartism. As Mr G. M. Young has said in his admirable *Portrait of An Age:*

> The failure of the New Poor Law to fulfil its promise, the inevitable harshness of a new administration suddenly applied to a people with no idea of administration at all, the brutality that went on in some workhouses and the gorging in others, the petty tyranny of officials and the petty corruption of Guardians, discredited the scientific Radicals and brought the sentimental Radicals to the front.

The new law brought a great change in the temper of the workers, no less than in the technique of administration:

these two changes, in combination, did much to set the tone of the next fifty years of English development.

Hot upon the footsteps of the new Poor Law came the overhaul of local government in the towns. In 1835 the Prisons Act established inspectors of prisons on the model of the inspectors of factories; the Poor Law deprived the parish vestries of their main functions; the repeal of the Test and Corporation Acts widened the basis of the borough corporations. County, parish, and borough authorities had all undergone some change of function within a few years. Interest centred first upon the borough, the least satisfactory of all the units of local government. The Reform Bill of 1832 removed some of the greatest disparities between them so far as parliamentary representation was concerned, but in most of them old closed corporations continued to wield local power. Again a Royal Commission was appointed to investigate the government of towns: and again a reform based on the twin principles of local representation and tighter central control was proposed. In 1835 the Municipal Reform Act instituted borough councils elected by the ratepayers as the regular form of town authority. Financial functions such as the floating of local loans required approval by the Treasury. These councils were to work through certain paid officials, at least the town clerk and the borough treasurer. They had power to make by-laws and exercised control over the police, municipal property, and some aspects of local finance – particularly the collection of rates. These changes, too, marked an extension of Whig and business interests into a realm hitherto often dominated by Tory and Anglican interests. As Dr Ivor Jennings remarks:

> The fundamental complaint of the Whigs was that the councils were dominated by Tories and Anglicans. The manufacturers and merchants who had brought wealth to the town, and had made

themselves wealthy in the process, thought themselves as good as their 'betters'. (*Principles of Local Government Law*, p. 47.)

The electorate of the new municipal councils included all householders who had occupied the property for three years and had paid the poor rate. This was normally narrower than the parliamentary electorate created by the Reform Bill of 1832, and narrower than that for the election of the Poor Law Guardians. The franchise was being made as complicated and anomalous as was the growing number of local authorities themselves. But it was wide enough to let into the municipal electorate most of the wealthier merchants and industrialists of the large towns. The reform substituted for the old corporations with exclusive interests and tendencies an organization of local residents for the purpose of satisfying their common needs.

Reform of Parliament

In all these ways – the organization of the new police, the new Poor Law, and the new municipal councils – the pattern of government in England was changed fundamentally within a single decade. In conjunction with the removal of religious disabilities, these reforms laid the structural foundations for a new kind of State in Britain: a State in which the electoral rights and civil rights of citizens were extended and given greater legal protection, but in which the ordinary citizen was subjected to a much greater degree of administrative interference, direction, and control from the centre. The most spectacular element in this whole process – the Reform Bill of 1832 – ensured that the new State should also be partially democratized at the centre. The full significance of 1832 in the history of the country is appreciated only if it is seen as the central change in this many-sided transformation of an agricultural nation ruled by squires, parsons, and wealthy landowners into an industrial nation dominated by the classes produced by industrial expansion and commercial enterprise.

The question of reforming the electoral basis of Parliament itself had long been in the air. Various proposals had been put forward during the previous sixty years. The actual Bill was the child of the Whigs, led by Lord John Russell and Earl Grey, and was a bitter disappointment to the Radicals such as Place. It carefully preserved the principle that it was property rather than persons which Parliament represented, although its official title suggested the contrary: 'an act to amend the representation of the people in England and Wales'. The extension of the franchise which it achieved was perhaps the less significant part of it: the £10 householder in the towns, the £10 copyholders and long leaseholders, the £50 short leaseholders and tenants-at-will in the counties, meant a total net addition of only 217,000 voters to the old electorate of 435,000. This was less than 50 per cent increase. Much more significant was the redistribution of seats among the constituencies. No less than 56 of the old rotten boroughs lost their separate representation, and 30 others lost one of their two members in the Commons. But representation was given to 42 other boroughs which had been without it, and these were in most cases the big new industrial and commercial towns of the north (Manchester, Birmingham, Sheffield, Leeds, and the rest) which had grown so greatly in recent years. The counties were also given 65 additional seats. The gross over-representation of the countryside and small agricultural towns was ended, and the new municipal middle classes of industry and business were given a more just share of power in constituting the House of Commons. Even so the conferring of the vote upon the £50 tenants-at-will in the counties retained ominous power for the landed interest:

because these men were the least independent and most easily influenced section of the county electorate. The Act instituted electoral registration as the necessary technical qualification for voting, and this not only opened a door to new and more intricate methods of corruption but also, in the long run, evoked more efficient party organization to ensure the inclusion of sympathizers on the registers. The absence of the secret ballot (which was not introduced until forty years later) left ample scope for pressure, victimization, and electoral disorders. The Eatanswill elections described in Dickens belong, it must be remembered, to the period after 1832. The discrepancy between the exaggerated hopes and lofty aspirations of those who backed the Bill and the realities of the Act's achievement betokened future instalments of reform: and that is perhaps the chief importance of the Act. It offered a taste of reform and whetted the appetite for more; it left abuses enough to provoke sustained agitation for another generation; but it set a precedent for changing even the most antiquated and traditionalist of institutions by legislative action. The methods of popular association and agitation which won so signal a victory in 1832 could be elaborated and refined, and become the basis of modern party organization. The conclusions drawn by the reforming movements were well expressed by a leader-writer of *The Times* two days after the final passing of the Reform Bill:

Many a green or grizzled jackanapes about the clubs, and public offices, and in Bond-street, was heard to declaim on the 'necessity of placing the "Hero of Waterloo" at the head of affairs', when the 'edge of the sword' would settle the question in a fortnight. We have our own doubts whether the 'Hero of Waterloo' would have resorted to such means, but none at all as to his utter discomfiture had he been hard-hearted or soft-headed enough to try them. But how did the people receive this disgusting language? Did it terrify them into Toryism – or exasperate them to violence? – or involve them in any course unworthy of respectable and honest citizens? Certainly not. They shed no blood: they attacked not the person of any public enemy. They only joined the Political Unions by myriads – attended meetings by 200,000 at a time – discussed public questions with more eagerness and ability than ever – and signed and presented fresh petitions to Parliament.

The manner in which the Bill passed through Parliament was important. Under the leadership of the Whigs, backed by intense popular pressure in the country which was mobilized for reform by men like Francis Place, it got through by the timely concession of Tories like Wellington and the standing threat that the King would swamp the Lords by the creation of new peers. It seemed to prove on one hand that the British Constitution was flexible enough to reform itself without revolution, and on the other that the tide of reform was on the flow, lapping the very highest quarters of the Constitution as well as the lowest, and likely to carry the nation far beyond the limited reforms achieved in the 1830s. These two conclusions were, as events would soon show, quite true. The Reform Bill was the centre-piece in the sequence of reforms, following fast upon the achievement of religious equality and the experiment of the new police, and leading immediately to the overhaul of the poor law and the municipal councils. All these reforms were accompanied by a corresponding series of changes in the commercial and fiscal policy of the country, and to these we must next turn before exploring the further political changes to which the Reform Bill and its accompaniments gave rise.

CHAPTER IV

ECONOMIC AND SOCIAL
REFORMS

Free Trade

To the forces of business enterprise, commercial and industrial, it seemed that the fiscal policy of England was as completely burdened by inefficient and out-of-date restrictions and regulations as were the legal and political systems of the country. They had a common interest in sweeping away the most irksome of these relics. In 1820 the London Merchants presented to Parliament a petition which embodied principles that were to win ascendancy in economic policy during the next forty years. Two of the most important of these were:

> That freedom from restraint is calculated to give the utmost extension to foreign trade, and the best direction to the capital and industry of the country.
>
> That the maxim of buying in the cheapest market and selling in the dearest, which regulates every merchant in his individual dealings, is strictly applicable as the best rule for the trade of the whole nation.

These principles which had been laid down forty-four years before by Adam Smith in *The Wealth of Nations* were now to reform British commercial and fiscal policy: their results, in combination, are usually called 'the free trade movement'. It was a movement in which some of the greatest names of the century, Cobden and Bright, Peel and Gladstone, were to take a leading share. In the period between 1815 and 1848 it began as a purely utilitarian and piecemeal movement, thriving on the mild modifications of import duties carried out by men like Huskisson: it ended as a doctrinaire force making for complete freedom of trade, backed by a whole philosophy of commercial liberalism and a new popular faith in the virtues of free competitive enterprise.

Commercial policy at this time was closely linked with two political considerations: the need to raise taxation in conditions where the land tax was the chief alternative source of revenue and income tax was a war-time novelty; and the urge to protect British shipping interests so that in case of war the British Navy should be strong. The countless and clumsy import duties and excises were imposed as much to raise revenue as to protect British industries, and the Navigation Laws, dating from 1651 and 1660, were intended to serve the double purpose of protecting British shipping and restricting the expansion of Britain's chief naval rivals. The trend of the reforms between 1820 and 1848 was to separate economic policy from political considerations, to mould it entirely in terms of promoting national wealth by untrammelled private enterprise, and to leave considerations of national defence and of taxation to the direct action of government through naval building and the imposition of income tax and other direct taxes. Some of the details of these trends are of special interest.

The first moves to simplify and diminish import duties came from the Liberal-Tory Ministries of the 1820s. Huskisson at the Board of Trade contrived to reduce or eliminate some of the more irksome duties. The total national revenue from Customs and Excise in the late 1820s was roughly £36,000,000 a year: all other sources of taxation yielded only some £13,000,000. The bulk of this Customs and Excise revenue came from duties on sugar, tea, coffee, beer and spirits, wine, and tobacco; some of it came from duties on the import of corn and timber and from excise duties on paper, glass, leather, printed calicoes, and muslins. When Huskisson consolidated and simplified the system of tariffs in 1824-5 he made no fundamental change of principle. In so far as bounties were still given – quite unnecessarily – on certain commodities exported or re-exported, these actually imposed a burden on revenue rather than contributing to it. Bounties came under first and heaviest fire from the free traders. The basic problem, in an age when, despite the *laissez-faire* doctrines of Benthamism, the State was beginning to do more and cost more, was how to find a better alternative source of revenue. The main alternative found was income tax, as part of a Property Tax. In 1803 a Property and Income Tax of 2s in the pound was imposed, but this was repealed when the wars ended. It was 1842 before Peel's budget revived Income Tax at the rate of 7d in the pound in Great Britain. Eleven years later it was extended to Ireland. It has never since disappeared from British budgets, and it soon became the chief source of inland revenue.

With this alternative source of revenue at the disposal of Government, Peel, and after him Gladstone, were able to repeal many of the old restrictive and wasteful duties. The budget of 1842 reduced the tariff on some 750 articles, and three years later Peel reduced tariffs still more. Duties on raw materials were mostly abolished, and those on manufactured articles were consolidated at a general level of 10 per cent. In these ways the burden of revenue was moved from trader to ordinary citizen, and the motive of protection was virtually abandoned. In one major respect protection survived – in the Corn Laws.

Because the Corn Laws purported to protect the agricultural interest, and because they had proved themselves inefficient even for this purpose, they became the main target for free-trade polemics. In 1839 the Anti-Corn-Law League was founded at Manchester by 'representatives from all the great sections of our manufacturing and commercial population.' The founders resolved that 'the agricultural proprietor, capitalist, and labourer are benefited equally with the trader, by the creation and circulation of the wealth of the country; and this meeting appeals to all those classes to cooperate for the removal of a monopoly which, by restricting the foreign commerce of the country, retards the increase of the population, and restrains the growth of towns; thus depriving them of the manifold resources to be derived from the augmenting numbers and wealth of the country.' From this beginning was launched the most sustained and intensive campaign of popular agitation which the first half of the nineteenth century had known. Throughout the country large mass-meetings were addressed by great popular orators of the calibre of John Bright and Richard Cobden. The doctrines of free trade, not only in their application to the Corn Laws but in their broadest philosophical implications for national prosperity, power, and peace, were disseminated. Through the agitation, the principles of free-trade liberalism were implanted deeply in the middle classes and in large sections of the labouring classes too. The ideological foundations of Victorian England were laid by the battle for cheaper bread – and for higher profits.

The background to the Anti-Corn-Law agitation was a series of bad harvests before 1842 and a severe trade depression which entitled the years from 1839 to 1843 to the label of 'the hungry forties'. It was contended that by raising the price of food and the cost of living, by reducing purchasing power and discouraging the export of manufactured goods in exchange for imported corn, the Corn Laws were causing public distress and ham-stringing foreign trade and home manufactures. Free trade became in the hands of Cobden and Bright a gospel, a cure for all social ills, and the path to international peace. They combined the *laissez-faire* philosophy of Bentham and the humanitarian philosophy of the philanthropists into one coherent and plausible set of doctrines, which were presented with remarkable vigour and lucidity to the mass of the people. It was distinct from the movement for 'freer trade' under Huskisson, and now became the gospel of the factory-owners and industrialists rather than of the merchants and shippers. After Sir Rowland Hill introduced the penny post in 1840 the League was able to use this new means of disseminating its propaganda: its normal methods of mass-meeting and popular oratory continued as well, and now that the respectable middle classes had adopted these traditionally radical modes of agitation they became a more regular feature of English political life. In his budget of 1842 Peel lowered the duty on corn. The climax came in 1845 when the potato crop in Ireland failed. Famine became imminent and there was a bad corn harvest in England. Sir Robert Peel, already moving towards the conviction that the Corn Laws would have to go, succeeded after a rapid run of ministerial crises in repealing the Corn Laws. He fell from power immediately afterwards, but the deed was done. The 'repeal' Act levied very low duties on corn, even when it was dear, so the old principle was not completely swept away. This duty was suspended in January, 1847, and remained suspended until March, 1848: after 1849 the duty remained at one shilling a quarter.

The whole controversy was conducted in very exaggerated terms and the importance both of the Corn Laws and of their repeal was inflated by the demagogic methods of the League. Prices did not fall greatly after repeal, and were still apt to be unstable for quite other reasons which had been ignored by the opponents of the Corn Laws. Most important of all was the example, which the whole campaign had offered, of how newly-won political power might be used to carry out economic reforms and advance certain economic interests. It was a lesson which the Chartists and later socialist movements were to learn with effect.

When Adam Smith first presented the full-dress case for free trade he had made an exception of the Navigation Laws on the grounds that 'defence, however, is of much more importance than opulence', and had called them 'perhaps the wisest of all the commercial regulations of England.' They excluded all non-British shipping from the carrying trade between England and her overseas possessions, and limited the import of foreign goods to ships of England or of the country from which the goods came. Even so, goods coming in ships of their own country incurred higher import duties. The elaborate system of discrimination which had been built up on these Laws was intended to protect the interests of British shipping and so, in time of war, to strengthen the British Navy. During the French Wars the restrictions had been enforced with some laxity and various detailed modifications had been introduced. Now that the Corn Laws had gone it was difficult for the shipping interests to defend these restrictions in their own favour: and anyhow many lost faith in them now that British shipping had such great natural superiority in the world. In 1849, accordingly, the Navigation Laws were in turn repealed, and a further set of artificial obstacles to free trade was removed.

In these ways the 1840s, which saw Peel's great budgets and the removal of Corn and Navigation Laws, tipped the scale still further away from special advantages for the agricultural interests towards a system which was particularly favourable to the industrial and commercial interests. The State was adjusting itself to the new balance of social forces, in economic policy no less than in politics and administration. The sequel was a period of unrivalled material prosperity for the country. In 1842 the value of British exports was slightly less than it had been in 1815 – some £47,250,000 as against £50,000,000. But twenty-eight years after Peel's budget, it had risen to £200,000,000. The middle generation of the century was, then, the era which made Britain indeed 'the workshop of the world'. At the same time farming prospered. Until the 1870s, when the products of North America began to compete with those of English farms, the middle generation knew agricultural revival and prosperity. Meanwhile, parallel to the rise of the Anti-Corn-Law League, there had arisen a highly significant movement among the lower-middle and working classes which throws further light on the problems of this first post-war generation. It is the movement of Chartism.

Chartism

The roots of the Chartist movement were partly political and partly economic. In part it was a consequence of the failure of Owen's experiments in trade unionism and of popular discontent with the moderation of the Reform Bill. Disillusioned elements of Owen's Union joined hands with radical movements among the well-to-do London artisans and with the movements of mass-discontent in Lancashire and Yorkshire. The last were motivated more by the economic distress and social exploitation of industrialism than by political ideologies. But all fused together to produce one of the most dynamic movements of working-class agitation so far known in England. As already mentioned, William Lovett founded the London Working Men's Association of respectable and self-educated artisans in 1836. Two years later he and Francis Place drew up the 'People's Charter' as the political programme of their society. It called for universal male (not female) suffrage; equal electoral districts; removal of the property qualification for members of Parliament; payment of members of Parliament; secret ballot; and annual general elections. The first five of these 'Six Points' have now become so much a part of our working parliamentary system that it is difficult to appreciate how radical they were in 1838. Their radical spirit comes out in the sixth point. Had a system of annual elections been permitted our political system would have become one of direct rather than parliamentary democracy.

Parliament is sovereign, both in the legal sense that it can pass any law about anything, and in the political sense that nothing the electorate can do can ensure the dismissal of a government or the dissolution of a Parliament before the end of its legitimate five-year period of power. A House of Commons subject to annual elections would be an instrument of direct democracy; and the effects which nineteenth-century men normally expected of the growth of democracy – abolition of the monarchy and of the House of Lords – would most probably have come to pass. The other five points, it must be remembered, were agreed to only very slowly and piecemeal during the years 1858–1918.

If the moderate demands of Lovett seemed more radical then than now, his movement was soon joined by forces which do not even appear moderate to us. There was, first, the Birmingham Political Union, dating from 1816, which was revived by Thomas Attwood (1783–1856). Attwood was something of a novelty – a very radical banker; though his views on currency made him very unorthodox even as a banker. The Birmingham Union sponsored the People's Charter and called for a National Petition on its behalf. This meant intensive drives of big public meetings, propagandist societies, and general popular agitation, and as such was distrusted by many of the Londoners who supported Lovett. The Chartist movement was joined, too, by a third. and still more demagogic movement, led by the hot-headed Irish landowner Feargus O'Connor (1794–1855), whose Leeds paper the *Northern Star* became the official Chartist organ. On this tripod basis – London, Birmingham, and Leeds – the Chartists organized big meetings all through the year 1838, some of them involving exciting torchlight processions at night, and most of them enabling the hungry, indignant, and often ignorant populace of the distressed northern counties to hear the fiery speeches of J. R. Stephens, James Bronterre O'Brien, and Richard Oastler. 'The Charter' became the battle-cry of a nation-wide movement, and something of a religion which was expected to bring universal relaxation.

The climax of the Chartist agitation was the National Convention which was gathered together in Westminster Palace Yard, very near the Houses of Parliament, in the spring of 1839. Its accompaniment was the organization of a monster petition for which hundreds of thousands of signatures were collected. The Convention was deeply split over what to do if Parliament should reject the petition. Lovett and his southern followers urged a further campaign of peaceful agitation and popular education: O'Connor and his northern supporters urged violent reprisals. A Polish exile published articles on revolutionary tactics, and pamphlets were sold on how best to build barricades. There was a tang of civil war in the air. In May the Convention moved to Birmingham, and in July the petition with nearly a million and a quarter signatures was rejected by the Commons. Despite the riots, local strikes, and even insurrection which accompanied these events, the firm wisdom of Lord John Russell as Home Secretary and the solid sense of the working-class artisans prevented anything worse.

During the 1840s the National Charter Association kept alive the principles of the movement, and in 1842 a second petition was presented and again rejected. In 1848 – the year of revolutions in Europe – a third petition was prepared and the movement fell increasingly into the hands of O'Connor and the extremists. So many of the alleged signatures were forged and the threatened monster procession to Parliament was such a fiasco that the whole movement petered out. Chartism in this second phase after 1839, although more violent in tone, was never so serious and solid a movement as in its earlier phase. The middle classes were diverted from interest in Chartism to support for the Anti-Corn-Law League; the artisans reverted to peaceful agitation; and large sections of the working classes began to turn to trade unionism. Latterly only the cranks, the rabble, and portions of the industrial wage-earners remained faithful to Chartism, and it came to an end in general apathy and ridicule, killed partly by reviving trade and greater prosperity. Although its chief aims were political and constitutional reforms, its roots lay in social and economic distress. It accepted the characteristic liberal doctrine that political reforms precede and determine social and economic improvement, and that universal suffrage would herald a new dawn of democratic society. But its periods of greatest activity coincide with periods of depression and distress, just as its intermissions and decline coincide with periods of reviving prosperity. The rise and fall of Chartism were a barometer of industrial and agricultural distress in England.

Its failure as a political movement was more apparent than real. Five of the six points were fully incorporated in due course into the working constitution of England by 1918. It drew the attention of all classes to the 'condition of England question', and that attention was never subsequently lost. John Stuart Mill's *Political Economy*, which appeared in 1848, showed how far radicalism was moving towards socialism. Distinguished literary men and women so concertedly turned their attention to social evils that the middle of the century saw a new era of 'social' literature. Thomas Hood's *Song of the Shirt*, Mrs Browning's *Cry of the Children*, Mrs Gaskell's *Mary Barton*, Charles Kingsley's *Yeast* and *Alton Locke*, Thomas Carlyle's *Chartism* and *Past and Present*, are all literary by-products of the Chartist commotion. A group of Christian Socialists, led by Charles Kingsley, F. D. Maurice, Thomas Hughes, and J. M. Ludlow, began to exert a strong influence on Anglican thought. And Disraeli, whose novels *Sybil* and *Coningsby* were directly prompted by his interest in social evils exposed by the agitation, was led to found the Tory Radical movement of 'Young England' which claimed an alliance between workers and aristocracy against the new commercial middle classes. By these channels a new and healthier wind blew through the community, a new national consciousness and social conscience about the ills of industrial England were begun, and the whole commotion severely shook the hardening complacency of the Victorian era. In these ways Chartism, routed in 1848, left a deep and permanent mark on English history. It was the first widespread and sustained effort of working-class self-help; it was directed to the cause of parliamentary democracy and constitutional reform; and the impetus it gave to eventual political reform on one hand and to trade union organization on the other was never wasted. All these three facts about it give it lasting importance.

Social Liberalism

The spirit which animated the political leaders of England during this first generation after Waterloo is shown at its best in two sets of measures affecting the peoples of the Empire. One is the abolition of slavery within the Empire: the other is the evolution of the ideal of responsible government, which gave rise to our modern notion of Dominion status. These achievements of the new spirit of radical liberalism were amongst its greatest and its most completely successful: and both involved a quality of mind, a generosity of policy, and a breadth of human sympathy which help to explain Britain's tremendous prestige in the world during the mid-Victorian era.

Moves for the abolition of slavery had been made by the younger Pitt in 1787 but, as with so many other projected reforms, the intervening wars had delayed any further progress. By 1807, however, Charles James Fox (1749–1806) had succeeded in getting the slave trade abolished within the British Empire. Punishment was imposed on British subjects who caught slaves or took part in the trade in slaves, and British ships persisting in that trade were liable to confiscation. Men like William Wilberforce, Granville Sharp, and Buxton followed this success with pressure to get foreign countries to abolish the trade, and by 1815 France, Spain, and Portugal had agreed to stop it. But extensive smuggling went on and the remaining trade was even more atrocious in the conditions it imposed on its victims than before. An Abolition Society, headed after 1818 by Buxton and Zachary Macaulay, proceeded to urge the abolition of slavery itself – a logical development of the ban on slave-trading but a step which was liable to cause much more dislocation, and arouse more bitter opposition, among the plantation-owners of the British colonies, particularly the West Indies. At first piecemeal improvements in the lot of the slaves were achieved, but these proved insufficient in the face of planters' resistance. In 1833 Stanley (1799–1869), backed by Buxton, got through Parliament his Act 'for the abolition of slavery throughout the British colonies.' All slaves were to be freed within a year, but those in agriculture were to remain apprenticed to their former masters until 1840. The British taxpayer bore the burden of meeting £20,000,000 compensation paid to the slave-owners – an average rate of £37 10s per slave. In 1838 the system of apprenticeship was abolished by the colonies. Although many radicals at home might with justice criticize the conscience of a ruling class which showed itself so tender for black slaves overseas but so tough for white 'free' labourers at home, in cotton mill and coal-mine, yet the decisive abolition of an age-old evil like slavery within a few years and at heavy national expense was a remarkable and noble achievement. It set the rest of the world an example; and in the end it killed slavery throughout the civilized world.

If the future of the British colonial Empire was determined by the timely abolition of slave-trade and slavery, the foundation of the British Commonwealth of Nations was laid within the same decade by the wise treatment of British North America. The loss of the American colonies fifty years before served as a warning that new methods of imperial government were called for if the rest of North America was not also to seek total separation from Britain. The forces which championed the movement for free trade favoured also a modification of British methods of colonial government, but they were divided over the kind of changes which should be made. Bentham, James Mill, and the older generation of radical thinkers opposed any effort to keep a hold over colonial territories, which they regarded as a burden and a cause of war. In 1836 Cobden compared them to the hated Corn Laws as 'merely accessories to our aristocratic government', and when free trade principles triumphed in 1842 he claimed that by loosening British colonial ties they would bring further advantages. The younger school of radicals, adhering less rigidly to *laissez-faire* principles, wanted a new liberal colonial policy which might succeed in preventing the further separation of colonies from the mother country. Sir William Molesworth (1810–55), John Stuart Mill, Lord Durham (1792–1840), Gibbon Wakefield (1796–1862) and Charles Buller (1806–48) groped their way towards a policy of liberal imperialism which bore fruit, in 1839, in Lord Durham's Report on Canada.

In 1791 Pitt's Act had divided the old Province of Quebec into two provinces of Upper and Lower Canada. Each of these provinces was equipped with the traditional apparatus of British colonial government – a representative assembly with control of legislation and taxation, a Governor appointed by the British Government in London, and an executive council nominated by the Governor. As in the American colonies in the eighteenth century there was apt to be friction between the assemblies on one hand and the Governors and executive councils on the other; for the latter owed responsibility not to the provincial assembly but to the British Government. In Lower Canada (Quebec) the assembly reflected the French majority in the province by being overwhelmingly French in composition, whereas the executive council was entirely British. There existed a highly precarious and inflammable situation throughout the British North American Colonies, with Quebec as the main danger point because of the nationalistic rivalry between the French and British populations. In 1837 the French and some disaffected British and Irish in both Upper and Lower Canada rebelled; the rebellion in Lower Canada, led by Louis Papineau, a demagogue, being much the more serious. In the following year when the rebellions had been crushed Lord Durham was sent out, as Governor and High Commissioner with wide powers, to inquire into the whole situation. He took out with him Wakefield and Buller, with whom in 1830 he had founded the Colonization Society. They approached the whole problem essentially from the point of view of how Canada could be made a safe, attractive, and prosperous home for British emigrants. Their remedy for the social ills and human distress of Britain was systematic colonization: emigration wisely directed into the most fertile parts of the empire which should be treated as a unity. Emigration of British citizens should not entail the loss of British citizens to the mother country: it should mean, instead, the systematic extension of the principles of parliamentary government to the colonies and the creation of a new imperial unity knit together by freedom, and by a common inheritance of political traditions. The concrete and urgent problem which confronted them was how these principles could be applied to the complex and difficult situation in the Canadian provinces. Durham's answer was given in his Report.

It includes a wealth of detail, now of little interest, concerning the proper use of public lands, emigration, communications, and so on. These serve only to emphasize how much Durham and his friends were concerned with better facilities for emigration. Wakefield's chief contribution to colonial theory was his linking of the two problems of how to prevent wasteful accumulation of land by colonists unable to make the best use of it, and how to enable desirable emigrants to overcome the financial obstacle of the costs of the journey. He urged that the Government should sell colonial land at a good price, not distribute it free: and that the proceeds should be used to help good emigrants to pay the costs of transport. He hoped that by these means the mother country and the colonies would become 'partners in a new industry, the creation of happy human beings.' These ideas found their place in Durham's Report.

But the recommendations for which it is memorable and historically important are its political principles: the re-union of Upper and Lower Canada into one Province, and the grant of responsible government to the united Province. He urged not federation but the complete fusion of the provinces, as a necessary prelude to the granting of responsible government and as essential for the strength and welfare of the inhabitants of both. To modern ears his advice sounds machiavellian and ruthless – 'to settle, at once and for ever, the national character of the province' by swamping the French colonists, by 'Anglifying' them as thoroughly as possible, and so ensuring a permanent British hegemony within the united province. Durham justified this policy by its end – self-government. 'At the root of the disorders of Lower Canada,' he wrote, 'lies the conflict of the two races which compose its population: until this is settled, no good government is practicable.' He saw that self-government depended on national unity – an important doctrine of later Gladstonian Liberalism but different in its application from the doctrines of 'national self-determination' held still later by President Wilson. He hoped, eventually, for a united British North America, built around the union of Upper and Lower Canada. Government should, secondly, be made responsible government. The executive officers should be made responsible to the legislature of the province, and no longer to the Colonial Office in London. To achieve this it was necessary only to 'follow out consistently the principles of the British Constitution. Administer the government on those principles which have been found perfectly efficacious in Great Britain.' Durham was pressing the principles of British parliamentary government much further than they had so far been pressed at home: in the year of his Report Chartism, as already shown, was beginning to demand a more democratic system and it was to fail in its immediate objectives. With remarkable insight and foresight he saw the direction in which British government was to develop within the next generation. By implanting these seminal principles in British colonial policy, and first in the actual constitution of Canada, he ensured the birth of the British Commonwealth of Nations. He held that responsible government, far from loosening the bonds of empire, would preserve its unity by making it a community of free nations, with a natural harmony of interests between its various parts. It was the veritable climax of optimistic liberalism – and has close affinities with Cobden's faith that international harmony and peace would naturally follow from free trade. Lord John Russell, the Prime Minister, did not share this extreme optimism: and Durham proposed in his Report that certain matters (the constitution of the provinces, the disposal of the public lands, the regulation of foreign relations and of trade with the mother country) should be reserved for the British Government. These reservations from full self-government were soon to break down, and the story of their break-down is the story of the evolution of full Dominion Status.

His Report was not fully implemented at once. In 1840 Upper and Lower Canada were re-united, and Poulett-Thomson (Lord Sydenham) was appointed Governor-General. His successors were less good, and by 1846, when Canada suffered from repeal of the Corn Laws, a serious crisis arose again. The following year Durham's son-in-law, Lord Elgin, became Governor-General. His period of rule, until 1854, saw the establishment in practice of responsible government, which thus rested not on statutory grant but on convention and practical arrangements. In 1867 the British North America Act opened the door for the federation of all the provinces except Newfoundland into Canada, and this federation was completed within the next six years. The union of 1840 was dissolved within the wider federation. Meanwhile the Canadian model was copied in New Zealand in 1854, Australia in 1856, and Cape Colony in 1872. In this very concrete sense the pattern of the present British Commonwealth of Nations dates from 1839.

The effect of the new colonial policy (reinforced in 1849 by the repeal of the Navigation Acts) was to facilitate emigration from the British Isles. The coming of railways and steamships facilitated travel at the same time as reception areas were being made more attractive, and as economic pressure at home was exerting an impulse to emigrate. The figures for 1830 show a sudden increase to 60,000 from the previous maximum of some 30,000 a year. In 1832 it was over 100,000, in 1842 it was 130,000. The annual average for the three years 1847–9 was well over 250,000. The export of men and women increased at this tremendous rate during the first generation after Waterloo, and nevertheless the population remaining in Britain also increased. It doubled between 1801 and 1851. It is noteworthy that the urge for the years around 1848 was that of famine in Ireland and hardship in England and Scotland. The 'push' was always more important than the 'pull': and in the years 1844–5, when corn was cheap, emigration slackened.

The main tide of this emigration rolled towards North America – to the United States and the Canadian provinces. It flowed also towards the antipodes. By 1840 Australia had some 130,000 white inhabitants, and prevailed upon Britain to end the bad habit of using the colony as a dumping-ground for convicts. Twenty years later the population was about one million. In 1837 Wakefield founded the New Zealand Association which made the first British settlements there. In Cape Colony the settlement of 5000 British immigrants in 1820 started the process of establishing British hegemony over Dutch Boer farmers which seemed likely to duplicate the story of the relations between French and British in Lower Canada. Boer grievances, culminating in their objection to the inadequate compensation given when slavery was abolished and to the British Government's tenderness towards raiding Kaffir tribes, led to the Great Trek in 1836. Several thousand Boer farmers and their families set out across the veldt with their ox-wagons to seek independence beyond the reach of the Cape government. They founded farmer republics on the Orange River and in Natal. Soon British expansion caught up with them, and in 1843 Natal was annexed. By 1851 a few thousand British immigrants were brought into the colony and it became the most British area of South Africa: three years later the Orange Free State, a Boer republic, was created. A temporary compromise was reached, but the recurrent disputes between British and Boers about native rights were to raise further disputes during the second half of the century.

The Position of Britain in 1848

In foreign relationships the period 1815–48 was a period of peace. Harriet Martineau called the years 1816–46 'the Thirty Years' Peace'. Britain enjoyed the benefits of that absence of major European wars which was secured partly by exhaustion after the long era of French wars, partly by the operations of the Congress System and the policy of repression carried out for so long by Prince Metternich of Austria. Under the leadership of Castlereagh, Canning, and Palmerston she gradually dissociated herself from the anti-liberal and anti-nationalist policies of the System, backed as it was by the Holy Alliance of the eastern dynasties. She championed the freedom of the Greeks, of the Latin American colonies, and of the Belgians. But she avoided any major hostilities herself. Subject to the same tides of economic forces and social movements as the rest of western Europe, her counterpart to the European revolutions of 1830 was the Great Reform Bill two years later; her counterpart to the successful revolutions of 1848 which rocked Europe was the petering out of Chartism and the new tide of emigration in the same year. She seemed to have found, in her supple parliamentary institutions and her monarchical traditions, a strange immunity from violent revolution. As explained above, the threat of violence, and at times even violence itself, was often there. Yet her governing classes showed greater tact, skill, and statecraft in evading revolution than those of most European countries; her middle classes found satisfaction in such adjustments of the traditional order as gave them freedom to seek wealth through the new medium of factory and machinery, railway and steamship; and her labouring classes inherited a respect and affection for the methods of self-help and constitutional agitation, as well as a spirit of patience and tolerance, which held them back from 'the red fool-fury of the Seine' – or of the Danube. All shared to some extent, however inequitably, in the growth of national prosperity. By the middle of the century the worst hardships of the new Poor Law had been overcome or partially forgotten, emigration had served as an outlet for the intense pressure of population on the economic resources of the country, and it was noted that workmen were wearing, perhaps for the first time in British history, very much the same sort of clothes as the gentleman. Such a country might well be envied by her European neighbours. But such a country was unlikely to find repose, or be able to prevent further great overhauls of her system of government and further immense changes in her way of life. A host of new forces had been launched upon the country. Far from having yet spent their force or revealed all their demands, they were just at the very height of the most restless and dynamic stage of their history. It was more symbolic than men knew that when the Prince Consort's idea of holding a Great Exhibition of the Works of Industry of all Nations reached fruition in 1850, it was decided to house it in Hyde Park in Paxton's gigantic house of iron and glass – the most durable and also the most fragile of Britain's industrial products.

Throughout the century one constant factor in Britain's relations with her neighbours and in her own sense of national security operated so effectively and so silently that few gave it much thought: the British Navy. Her naval power grew steadily during the Napoleonic Wars, and by 1815 she had some 250 ships of the line, of which 100 to 150 were in commission. During the Wars she had captured from the French 113 ships of the line and 205 frigates, and most of these had gone to swell the size of her own Navy. It has remained something of a mystery to historians that with ill-disciplined officers and mutinous crews, often recruited by the brutal methods of the press-gang, British naval power stood so high even in the time of Nelson. Already before 1815 the Navy suffered eclipse in popularity, and the Army under Wellington held the stage. The financial economies after 1815, the paying-off of some 120,000 sailors, the refusal until as late as 1853 to make a rule of offering continuous service to seamen rather than single commissions for each ship, brought the Navy into a remarkable state of decline. The greater part of the fleet was laid up for almost a generation after Waterloo. Because of the ultra-conservative outlook of the higher command and the senior officers the adoption of more up-to-date designs and methods of construction and equipment was slow. As with the Army, experience of the Crimean War and the growth of armaments in other European States brought some improvements. The first iron-clad, the *Warrior*, was launched in 1860, and naval estimates were increased. The use of iron for building ships and of steam for driving them came in slowly: but it came. As Professor E. L. Woodward has said:

> The transition from sail to steam, from wood to iron and shot to shell, from the chequered ships of Nelson's time to the turrets and protective armour of the navy of modern times, contrasted ominously with the hopes of philosophers and the popular idealism of the Great Exhibition. (*The Age of Reform*, p. 284.)

In the fifties and sixties, despite her great technological lead in industry and her vast merchant navy, Britain did not originate any of the great naval developments. She imitated changes introduced by France and America; and imitated so clumsily that naval shipbuilding passed through a *baroque* phase. The *Warrior*, for example, though built of iron, was a full-rigged steam-and-sail ship with three masts and a bowsprit, carrying her guns on the broadside. But Britain throughout the heyday of mid-Victorian prosperity kept up a large and costly fleet – the biggest in the world: and thereon she implicitly pinned her faith for complete national defence. The fleet in being was a permanent factor in her whole position, both in Europe and as a maritime Empire. It was even the framework for her policy of free trade, for it and nothing else ensured for all the freedom of the seas.

CHAPTER V

MID-VICTORIANISM

Material Progress

ON 1 May 1851, the Crystal Palace was opened by Queen Victoria. The following morning *The Times* wrote:

> There was yesterday witnessed a sight the like of which has never happened before, and which, in the nature of things, can never be repeated ... In a building that could easily have accommodated twice as many, twenty-five thousand persons, so it is computed, were arranged in order round the throne of our SOVEREIGN. Around them, amidst them, and over their heads was displayed all that is useful or beautiful in nature or in art. Above them rose a glittering arch far more lofty and spacious than the vaults of even our noblest cathedrals. On either side the vista seemed almost boundless ... Some saw in it the second and more glorious inauguration of their SOVEREIGN; some a solemn dedication of art and its stores; some were most reminded of that day when all ages and climes shall be gathered round the throne of their MAKER; there was so much that seemed accidental and yet had a meaning, that no one could be content with simply what he saw ... all contributed to an effect so grand and yet so natural, that it hardly seemed to be put together by design, or to be the work of human artificers.

These words could have applied equally to the mood of mid-Victorian England itself. The same year saw the appearance of Mrs Gaskell's *Cranford*, Mr Herbert Spencer's *Social Statics*, Sir Edwin Landseer's *Monarch of the Glen*. Sir Robert Peel had died the year before, the Duke of Wellington died the year after. The opening of the Great Exhibition was also the opening of the golden age of Victorianism, in the proper and essential meaning of that word. Even Thackeray, who only three years before had declared himself 'a Republican but not a Chartist', wrote odes to the Crystal Palace. London had become, if not the hub of the universe, at least the focus of the world.

The background of mid-Victorianism is growing material prosperity, and a level of industrial production and foreign trade which set England far ahead of all other countries. The elemental facts speak for themselves. The enclosure of common land, stimulated by the General Enclosure Act of 1845, proceeded apace. It was checked only in the late sixties by the resistance of the urban population, acting through the Commons Preservation Society, to their exclusion from the nearby countryside. The cultivated land of Britain grew three-quarters of the corn that she needed. The small farmer still survived in large numbers: in 1851, there were 90,000 farms of between five and forty-nine acres. Roughly half the agricultural acreage of England and Wales was cultivated by farms ranging in size from fifty to three hundred acres. The landlords of the big estates took great pride in them and spent much capital on improving them. Improved methods of stock-breeding, draining and manuring, machine ploughing, reaping and threshing, brought great prosperity to agriculture. The gold discoveries of the fifties, combined with the peace of the sixties, brought high prices and plentiful labour to the farmers.

The building of railways was continued. In 1848 Britain produced half the pig iron of the world, and proceeded to treble her output during the next thirty years. This output was partly absorbed by the great new shipbuilding industries, and British steamships, built first of iron and then of steel, dominated the seas in this period. By 1870 the foreign trade of the United Kingdom was more than that of

France, Germany, and Italy together, and nearly four times that of the United States. She was reaping the rich advantages of the lead she had gained by reason both of her political stability and of her industrial revolution and inventiveness. Material progress seemed, as by some new law of nature, to have been showered without stint on a people who rated industriousness, business efficiency, and private enterprise among the major virtues.

This situation induced in large sections of the upper and middle classes a mood of comfortable complacency which later generations have found the most unattractive of Victorian characteristics. But it induced also a mood of revolt and reaction against such complacency. If Lord Palmerston, Lord Macaulay, and Samuel Smiles are 'typical' of the mid-Victorian outlook, so also are Charles Dickens, Matthew Arnold, and Thomas Carlyle. The self-satisfaction usually found expression in a robust, if somewhat swaggering, attitude which found reflexion in both domestic and foreign policy. The cocksure pugnacity of Palmerston had at least a solid basis in material wealth, impregnable financial strength, and a strong fleet.

Samuel Smiles's *Self-Help* (which appeared in 1859, sold 20,000 copies that year and another 130,000 during the next thirty years) was rapidly succeeded by works with similar pious titles – *Thrift*, *Character*, *Duty* – which form a veritable catalogue of the Victorian 'virtues'. This long series of smug lay sermons on the virtues of industry and honesty, connecting always the practice of such virtue with the reward of material prosperity, is the shoddiest side of the mentality of the time. It was the instinctive creed of the prosperous industrialists and business men whose ethics now dominated English manners as they dominated English economic life. It found its enemy in Matthew Arnold's bitter attacks on barbarians and philistines. His *Culture and Anarchy* appeared just ten years after *Self-Help*. It is worth recalling that the finest exposition of Victorian Liberalism, with its breadth of humanity and sensitive honesty of spirit – John Stuart Mill's essay *On Liberty* – appeared in the same year as *Self-Help:* and so did Charles Darwin's *Origin of Species*. It is wiser but more difficult to try to understand mid-Victorianism than to ridicule it.

The idea of Progress was steadily creeping into the imagination of Englishmen during the generation after Waterloo. It was when he travelled in the first train from Liverpool to Manchester that Tennyson, believing that the wheels ran in grooves, wrote the line:

> Let the great world spin for ever down the ringing grooves of change.[1]

Twelve years later, when it appeared enshrined in *Locksley Hall*, we find many similar declarations of faith in the rapid progress of mankind. 'Better fifty years of Europe than a cycle of Cathay': that was the general sentiment of thoughtful mid-Victorians. With the ever-greater use of steam-power and machinery would come universal peace. Tennyson versified Cobden's prosaic dream:

> For I dipt into the future, far as human eye could see,
> Saw the Vision of the world, and all the wonder that would be;
> Saw the heavens fill with commerce, argosies of magic sails,
> Pilots of the purple twilight, dropping down with costly bales; . . .
> Till the war-drum throbb'd no longer, and the battle flags were furl'd
> In the Parliament of man, the Federation of the world.

When the Prince Consort spoke at the Mansion House a few weeks before the opening of the Great Exhibition he used it as the symbol of the forthcoming unity of mankind. 'We are living,' he said, 'at a period of most wonderful transition, which tends rapidly to accomplish that great end

1. cf. *Tennyson*, Memoir by his Son, Vol. I, p. 195.

to which indeed all history points – the realization of the unity of mankind.' The *Edinburgh Review*, reviewing the *Official Catalogue* of the Exhibition, described its aim as being 'to seize the living scroll of human progress, inscribed with every successive conquest of man's intellect.' The morning of its opening was described by *The Times* as 'the first morning since the creation of the world that all peoples have assembled from all parts of the world and done a common act.' Such was the buoyant, optimistic, and somewhat arrogant mood of 1851.

This mood, which seems almost to have been born in 1851, lasted for the next twenty years. It permeated much of the literature, history, art, and philosophy of these years: and if it also bred its own antidote and antithesis, the impact of the reaction against it was not felt very acutely until after 1870. It remains to examine a few of the more significant manifestations of this spirit in the thought and achievements of the time.

It was natural, and perhaps inevitable, that Victorian England should demand and find a historian of suitable temper and calibre to re-interpret English history in the light of her new prosperity. She found him in Lord Macaulay, just as she found her representative Poet Laureate in Lord Tennyson. A man of wide practical political and administrative experience, he brought his peculiarly masculine and self-confident mind to the writing of English history in a manner most compelling to his contemporaries. When the first two volumes of his *History of England* appeared in 1848 some 13,000 copies were sold in four months: when the third and fourth volumes followed in 1855, 26,500 copies sold in ten weeks. His robust and pictorial style, his vivid imagination, and above all his inherent Whiggery, appealed strongly to his time. His collected essays, mostly elaborate book-reviews, had been published some years earlier and established his reputation as an historian of shrewd, forceful, and pugnacious qualities. He never hid his strong prejudices. He detested Roman Catholicism as much as Jacobinism, and distrusted kings as much as mobs. As a fair spokesman of the middle classes, parliaments are his real heroes, though he was strongly attracted by the daring of men like Clive and Hastings. The Whig Revolution of 1688 and the Whig Reform Bill of 1832 are the events which most rouse his whole-hearted enthusiasm. Although he is more critical of the great Whigs of history, and more sympathetic to the Tories, than many of the opponents of the 'Whig interpretation of history' would believe, he nevertheless founded the popular 'Whig legend' of English history which during the rest of the nineteenth century sank deep into Englishmen's view of their own development.

Macaulay characteristically began his *History* with the hint that

> the general effect of this chequered narrative will be to excite thankfulness in all religious minds, and hope in the breasts of all patriots. For the history of our country during the last hundred and sixty years is eminently the history of physical, of moral, and of intellectual improvement.

He had an unconcealed delight in the material progress of England since 1688: he cannot describe the landing of William III at Torbay in 1688 without lingering in detail over the size, villas and other 'improvements' on view in Torbay in 1848. A more serious defect is that foreshortening of political development which tends to present the Whigs or their earlier 'counterparts' as always on the side of 'progress' and therefore always in the event 'right', and the Tories or their 'counterparts' as always against 'progress' and so always in the event 'wrong'. The tendency to identify right with success and Whiggery with progress is typically mid-Victorian. It is fair to add that Hallam went even further in this respect than Macaulay, and that with all his shortcomings Macaulay did more than any other writer to make the Englishman familiar with his own history. Despite the mass of research since carried out, and despite the prejudices which are obvious enough to be easily discounted, Macaulay's history remains a great classic and a vivid, living presentation of English history.

Equally typical of the mid-Victorian mind is H. T. Buckle's *History of Civilization*, which appeared fast on the footsteps of Macaulay's fourth volume. It was an attempt to handle human society by the methods of the physical sciences: to trace a casual connexion between climate and forms of social organization, size of population, and even the production and distribution of ideas. Natural grandeur stifles thought, and rationalism is a product of the plains. The materialistic assumptions underlying this interpretation of history need little emphasis: they, too, were very acceptable to the climate of opinion in Great Britain of the Great Exhibition.

Application of the ideas and conclusions of the physical sciences to the social sciences was an obvious procedure when the physical sciences had produced so many marvels. Walter Bagehot (1826–77) produced *Physics and Politics: Thoughts on the Application of the Principles of Natural Selection and Inheritance of Political Society*. This significant essay, an aftermath of Darwinism, discussed the forces providing survival value in a society, and defined the chief of them as the 'cake of custom' which that society forms, the spirit of conformity and social discipline, the 'legal fibre', which hold society together. But the stability thus produced would stifle progress, were it not that the 'cake of custom' gets broken, inaugurating an 'age of discussion' and replacing instinct by conscious intelligence. Herbert Spencer (1820–1903) also applied Darwinian conceptions to the social sciences, but in a different manner. He regarded the State as the enemy of man, and was an extreme individualist in politics. He tried to connect mental, moral, and social development directly with evolution, and identified evolution with progress. The survival of the fittest meant survival of the best. Spencer's main publications, *Man versus the State* (1884) and *The Principles of Ethics* (1891-3), belong to the last decades of the century, and he remained an almost lone figure championing the most extreme doctrines of *laissez-faire* long after most serious thinkers had abandoned them. Yet by insisting that the State and society should be thought of as organisms, subject to almost biological laws of evolutionary change, he prepared the way for a highly anti-individualist conception of the State, in which the individual parts can be treated as subordinate to the whole. The importance of Bagehot and Spencer, as of Buckle, in Victorian thought lies in their materialistic explanations of human and social development.

Yet it would be highly misleading to over-emphasize the materialism of mid-Victorian thought. It was uplifted by two other very powerful forces which were every bit as intrinsic to Victorian thought as was its materialism. One is religion, which played a very large part in mid-Victorian life and thought: the other is the generous humanitarian impulses which derived partly from evangelical religion, partly from liberalism. The prevalent pride in material progress and prosperity, which led to complacency and an implicit faith in systematic 'improvement', was partly offset by a genuine religious faith, by conscience, and by humility before the mystery of creation. The mid-Victorians were pre-eminently a Bible-reading, church-going, sabbatarian generation. They took their religion and their church-going as seriously as their production of greater wealth: though often not more seriously.

Moral Conscience

No interpretation of mid-Victorianism would be sound which did not place religious faith and observance in the very centre of the picture. The most generally accepted and practised form of Christianity at the time was that which may be broadly called evangelicalism, with its emphasis upon moral conduct as the test of the good Christian. In this sense it transcended all barriers of religious sect, and marked the religious outlook of a Quaker like Bright and of a High Churchman like Gladstone, a Low-Church Tory like Shaftesbury and a Presbyterian like Livingstone. It even coloured the outlook of an agnostic like T. H. Huxley and a man like Disraeli, who although Jewish by race was a practising Christian. Its basis was biblical. Bible-reading in the home was as popular as sermonizing in church. Its highest virtue was self-improvement. Its emphasis lay not on sacraments or ritual, but on organized prayer and preaching, and on the strict observance of Sunday. Until the 1870s this form of religion and of religious worship remained the normal form for the great mass of Englishmen, although they remained divided formally into Anglicans, Methodists, Presbyterians, Quakers, and the many other nonconformist sects. It was the period when the so-called 'nonconformist conscience' permeated English life and manners – even amongst conformists. Gradually it was weakened by the growth of free-thinking and rationalist movements connected with the development of scientific thought, by the growth of facilities for luxury and pleasure and of greater indulgence in these facilities, and by the more ritualistic, Anglo-Catholic movement connected with the names of John Henry Newman and Edward Pusey.

The chief characteristic, indeed, of the Church of England in the mid nineteenth century was its remarkable variety and comprehensiveness in belief. It comprised almost as wide a range of beliefs as did English society itself, and was in that sense at least a truly national Church. In 1846 the Evangelicals formed the 'Evangelical Alliance', which united all English Protestants, Anglicans, and Nonconformists alike, in a common resistance to Roman Catholicism and all its influences. They revived the missionary spirit. Their Church Missionary Society, dating from 1798, could by 1848 claim to have converted 10,000 Negroes in Sierra Leone, the whole Maori population of New Zealand, and 20,000 Indians. David Livingstone was at work in Africa. But during the thirties there had appeared a growing split between all sections of Anglican opinion under evangelical influence and the new High Church Tractarian movement. From 1833 onwards John Henry Newman (1801–90), John Keble, Edward Pusey, and Richard Froude, all Fellows of Oriel College Oxford, created by their writings and sermons what came to be known as 'the Oxford Movement'. Their 'Association of Friends of the Church' and the *Tracts for the Times* which they published in the thirties strove to revive the doctrine of apostolic succession as the basis of the Church's authority. The Oxford Movement began as an attack on Liberal tendencies within the Church, and its effect was to drive Evangelicalism into closer connexion with nonconformity. Its opponents denounced it as Romanism in disguise, and in 1845 Newman in fact joined the Roman Church, into which many of his friends followed him. Pusey and Keble remained, and within the Anglican Church continued to assert the importance of clerical office, vestment, and ritual. The increasing emphasis on ritualism led to liturgical warfare within the Church. The external effect was to rouse intenser public interest in ecclesiastical and religious matters. The eventual effect within the Church itself was the triumph of the Broad

Church party, or the Liberals. When the violent theological disputes subsided, it was characteristic of the times that Latitudinarianism held the field. As Élie Halévy has said:

> The Broad Church was not a definite party like the other two, with its associations, its organized propaganda, and its press. It was simply a direction of opinion, a tendency, we might even say in the widest sense of the term a group, within which several subordinate groups may be more or less roughly distinguished. (*A History of the English People*, vol. IV, p. 316.)

The sensational conversions to Rome were but self-exclusions from what remained the broadly acceptable national Church: though it is important to remember that half of the regular church-goers in this golden age of church-going were nonconformists. The religious census of 1851 revealed that of 7,261,915 people who attended a place of religious worship on 30 March 1851, only 3,773,474 attended Anglican churches.

One further internal result of the Oxford Movement and the theological controversies to which it gave birth was the rise of the movement which came to be known as 'Christian Socialism'. It was Liberal in tendency and led by F. D. Maurice (1805–72) and Charles Kingsley. They began, in 1854, their series of *Tracts for Priests and People*, concerned with current social problems: and thus religious fervour was again directed towards social and material 'improvement'. They sponsored the cause of better education for women, adult schools, and working men's colleges. Both, it may be noted, were sons of clergy and both became professors of history in universities. They tried to Christianize education, just as Thomas Arnold at Rugby taught the great ideal of the Christian gentleman to the public schools. Kingsley's novels – *Yeast* (1848), *Alton Locke* (1850) – taught his public about social problems and stirred their consciences about ills which Chartism had failed to remedy. His 'Socialism' was little more than a fervent humanitarianism, and he is more in the tradition of the great evangelicals of the earlier part of the century than in tune with the liberal radicalism of his own day. The Professor of History who could write *The Water Babies* and *Westward Ho!* is nevertheless an outstanding addition to the long list of remarkably versatile mid-Victorians. The Christian Socialists took a kindlier view of the after-life and of the Deity than their Oxford contemporaries. To a church-going public used to lurid descriptions of the tortures of Hell, Maurice denied belief in everlasting damnation: for which offence he fell into violent controversy with Pusey, and in 1853 was deprived of his professorship at the recently-founded King's College, London. The fervour of the Oxford Movement and of the Christian Socialists, and the *furore* caused by both, remain inexplicable unless it be remembered how deep was the mid-Victorian respect for religious belief.

Secondly, and often in close harmony with religion, the faith and philosophy of Liberalism helped partly to offset the powerful materialistic forces of mid-Victorianism. In William Ewart Gladstone (1809–98) Victorian Liberalism found a magnificent leader who was also a High Churchman with as strong a taste for theology as for politics. Between 1846 and 1874 no Conservative ministry ruled England for more than sixteen months at a time: and the total duration of non-Liberal ministries during these twenty-eight years was less than five years all told. Throughout the years 1852–68 Gladstone and Disraeli alternated as Chancellors of the Exchequer: after that they alternated as Prime Ministers. In governmental policy and administration mid-Victorian England was, therefore, an era of virtual Liberal hegemony: and until 1865 its greatest conservative force was the arch-Whig, Palmerston. Apart from the episode of the Crimean War (1854–6) it was for Britain a period of peace, broken only by turbulent but remote events like the Indian Mutiny and the Chinese war. In this it was characteristic of the whole Victorian era, for Britain took part in no major European war between 1815 and 1914. The background of localized disputes and brief, short-lived wars affecting mainly backward peoples, is an essential element in the Victorian outlook. The age of general European wars, such as those against Spain, against Louis XIV, and against Napoleon, seemed to be at an end. Only after 1900 did even the notion of another general European war loom above the horizon, although the antics of Napoleon III, Emperor of France after 1851, caused temporary alarms in London. The Great Peace seemed to die with the Great Queen in 1901: meanwhile Lord Palmerston could bluster against tyrannies and Disraeli could assert British prestige in the world at very low cost.

Not least of Britain's achievements during the fifty years after Waterloo was to assert her role as the exemplar and pattern of free constitutional government; a role which she had enjoyed for fifty years after 1715, partially lost during the thirty years before the French Revolution, and now recovered in fuller measure under Victoria. During the last decades of the eighteenth century men learned to look to America and to France for intellectual and moral leadership in the practice of liberal ideas: after 1815 they again learned to look to Britain as the model of stable and constitutional government, a safe refuge for exiles and defeated rebels and a stout champion of suppressed nationalities in Europe. If Palmerston sometimes overdid the part – as over the Don Pacifico incident in 1850[1] – or if Britain plunged unprepared into ill-considered hostilities as in the Crimean War, even this kind of self-assertiveness had a strong appeal to Englishmen at the time. It was left to Gladstone to re-

1. See below, p. 154.

interpret a liberal foreign policy as a combination of support for small and oppressed nationalities in the Balkans with a willingness to submit Britain's just claims to arbitration, as in the eventual settlement of the *Alabama* dispute with the United States in 1871. At home Liberalism meant increasing assumption by the State of responsibility for the social welfare and security of the citizen, and abandonment of the amoral doctrines of *laissez-faire* – 'devil take the hindmost'.[1]

Above all, mid-Victorian England was great enough to breed and nourish its own critics. Self-criticism could never be quite dormant so long as a Matthew Arnold or a Charles Dickens held so much of the public attention. Matthew Arnold (1822–88), son of the famous Dr Thomas Arnold of Rugby, is perhaps the finest critic of his day. Thoroughly Liberal in upbringing and temperament, he had, no less than the High Churchman Gladstone, a profound sense of religion. His *Culture and Anarchy* (1869) remains the most biting indictment of the materialism and bad taste of his times.

> What he did was to use certain anarchical tendencies and lawless incidents of his own day, due to a temporary phase of intense political excitement, as illustrations of the deep-seated *spiritual* anarchy of the English people, an anarchy which expressed itself in its hideous sprawling industrial cities, its loud-voiced assertion of personal liberty, its dismal, stuffy, and cantankerous forms of Christianity, its worship of size and numbers and wealth and machinery generally, its state-blindness, and its belief in collision (collision of parties, of sects, of firms) as the only way of salvation. (J. Dover Wilson: Introduction to *Culture and Anarchy*, p. xxxiii.)

Arnold was a liberal critic of Liberalism. He attacked the social, moral, and aesthetic evils which were the consequences of the materialistic, economic, and political

1. The results of Liberalism in domestic policy are considered below, Chapters VI–VII.

Liberalism of the mid nineteenth century. Here he joined hands with Newman.

> Liberalism prevailed; it was the appointed force to do the work of the hour; it was necessary, it was inevitable that it should prevail ... But what was it, this Liberalism, as Dr Newman saw it, and as it really broke the Oxford Movement? It was the great middle-class Liberalism, which had for the cardinal points of its belief the Reform Bill of 1832, and local self-government, in politics; in the social sphere, free-trade, unrestricted competition, and the making of large industrial fortunes; in the religious sphere, the Dissidence of Dissent and the Protestantism of the Protestant religion. (*Culture and Anarchy*, p. 62.)

It was the force he called Philistinism, as distinct from the attitude of the aristocracy ('The Barbarians') and from that of the 'vast residuum' ('The Populace'). There is no more erosive criticism of mid-Victorianism than Arnold's famous description of the characteristics of these three social classes.

> The graver self of the Barbarian likes honours and considerations; his more relaxed self, field-sports and pleasure. The graver self of one kind of Philistine likes fanaticism, business, and money-making; his more relaxed self, comfort and tea-meetings. Of another kind of Philistine, the graver self likes rattening; the relaxed self, deputations, or hearing Mr Odger speak. The sterner self of the Populace likes bawling, hustling, and smashing; the lighter self, beer. (*ibid*, p. 107.)

Is this analysis substantially untrue of twentieth-century England? Certainly the materialism of Victorianism, which Arnold attacked, did not die with Victoria.

Charles Dickens (1812–70) through his long series of immensely popular novels touched people's hearts and imaginations where Arnold touched only their intellects. His satires on poor law institutions, Chancery, and judicial procedure in general, profiteering private schools, and many other social ills of his times are well known. Having been a poor boy himself he had an instinctive and burning sympathy with the poor. He gloried in the broad humanity, the patience, good-nature, and good-humour of the poor, even while laughing at their foibles, conceits, and oddities. His significance is not that he propounded any programme of social reforms or political improvements, but simply that he painted, for all to appreciate and enjoy, a vivid picture of working class folk whose poverty could be seen not as a penalty from heaven or the punishment of sin, but as the product of bad social conditions and the consequence of man's inhumanity. He helped to dissolve the older and more wooden class-divisions of Victorian England, to awaken a broader and more humane interest in fellow-men, and to blow away in gusts of laughter many of the stuffy absurdities of outdated modes of thought. His remedy was Christian charity and good-natured benevolence, and he has been well described as 'nearer to Father Christmas than to Karl Marx.'

Thomas Carlyle (1795–1881) was a more violent and virulent critic than either Arnold or Dickens. He was above all a moralist, and a Puritan moralist at that, and thus he embodied more of the spirit of his times than he would have cared to admit. He was evangelical to the core. But this only gained for his savage denunciations a more ready and attentive hearing among his contemporaries. A decade and more before Disraeli in *Sybil* wrote of 'the two nations', Carlyle wrote of the division into 'Dandies and Drudges', by which he meant also rich and poor. This fundamental social cleavage was a problem which haunted all the critics of Victorianism, from Dickens to Karl Marx. It drove Carlyle to sympathy with the Chartists so far as they wanted to destroy the poverty of the poor. Disillusioned, he latterly turned more and more to the vague hope of salvation through a young man or an aristocracy of the wise. But these were the resorts of an old man, and the true Carlyle was as radical as Dickens, filled with a burning hatred of poverty, cruelty, and man's inhumanity to man.

That these great – and many lesser – critics were able to find so wide a hearing was characteristic of Victorian times, and the best refutation of the slander that the mid-Victorians were incorrigibly complacent. Professor E. L. Woodward has suggested that 'against the background of an earlier age the Victorian era appears as a vast and unexpected awakening of conscience and an attempt, however imperfect, to apply the Christian ethic to modern conditions.' Later generations have come to regard as man-made and intolerable many things which the Victorians accepted as without remedy. The Victorians regarded as intolerable many other things which their ancestors had deemed without remedy, and they had slowly to invent appropriate means to deal with these new-found but not novel social evils. If they exaggerated the amount of good that would come from removing official controls, that was not because they were indifferent to social evils but because the administrative machinery through which old controls had to work was so unbelievably complicated, corrupt, and inefficient. As the Victorians groped their way towards more efficient and flexible methods of administration they proved ready enough to assume collective responsibility for tackling the worst social evils of their time. Evils felt to be humanly remediable were tackled as promptly, and, on the whole, as competently, as the means at their disposal allowed. The organized improvement of working-class housing, of factory conditions, of public health, of education, came remarkably fast once appropriate devices and scientific knowledge became available.

It is, indeed, part of the eternal greatness of the Victorian era that Englishmen showed themselves so energetically persistent and so ingeniously inventive in discovering better ways of improving social conditions. There could be no efficient drainage system or water supply until they had invented the cheap pipes and the traps and gullies which were hitherto unknown. Modern plumbing was characteristically a mid-Victorian invention, and received the enthusiastic support of a man like Edwin Chadwick whose Benthamism, as already shown, was the opposite of *laissez-faire*. Where the Victorians became laughable was in their over-enthusiastic adoption of new devices – such as upholstery, made possible by the invention of cheap metal springs. The once beautiful furniture of the eighteenth century was padded, sprung, and upholstered until it lost all recognizable shape or beauty. Houses and cottages, formerly made by necessity out of local materials which naturally harmonized with the soil and the landscape, were now made of red bricks, Welsh slate, cheap foreign softwoods, and cheap cement, which new methods of cheap and speedy transport made it possible to fetch from any part of the country to any other. Old and well-tried local craftsmanship broke down, established traditions and methods gave way to mass-produced work assembled by semi-skilled labour. Public taste, dominated by the upstart classes of the new rich, was as bad as Matthew Arnold described it. Beauty was killed in village after village, town after town, house after house, by this powerful combination of new amenities and low public taste. This is one of the biggest crimes of the mid-Victorians, even if they can scarcely be blamed for it. In material construction, as in public administration, they had to experiment with untried methods and evolve new techniques; and it is less surprising that they made hideous mistakes than that they made such speedy progress in refining and adapting the techniques.

Victorian art and architecture suffered from similar afflictions. The Crystal Palace was one of the very few attempts at functional architecture. The Albert Memorial is a fair enough sample of Victorian notions of decoration and monumental architecture. Sculpture and painting were traditionally tied to the art of representation: their social basis was the need to create a recognizable likeness of some-one or something. The invention of photography in the Victorian era introduced a technique of accurate repre-sentation with which sculpture and painting could not compete, and they were therefore free to abandon the effort to produce mere likeness and to concentrate on artistic creation. But both remained haunted by the old tradition, and the new school of impressionists, led by the American artist, Whistler, made slow pregress at first. Yet art criticism enjoyed a remarkable vogue, as evidence the enormous in-fluence of John Ruskin, and in the Pre-Raphaelite move-ment of Dante Gabriel Rossetti, Holman Hunt, and G. F. Watts the age produced a characteristic criticism of tradition whilst remaining 'naturalistic'. And in music the era was more creative. A particularly English school of music was founded by men like Sterndale Bennett, Parry, Stanford, Mackenzie, and Sullivan, though the Royal College of Music was not founded until 1883. The long series of comic operas by Gilbert and Sullivan began in the late seventies, and is a characteristically middle-class product of the period, laughing robustly at peers and pirates alike.

The industrial and commercial classes which, by reason of their wealth and their control of economic life, came to dominate English society and culture in the middle decades of the century, stamped upon English development an impress peculiarly their own. At once materialist and moral, aggressive and religious, self-satisfied and self-critical, the middle generation of Victorians enjoyed a special moment in English history. Their final achievement is that they were liberal enough in mind to extend the amenities and advantages of their creation to classes poorer and less organized than themselves, and to do this without bloodshed. Like the Whig aristocracy of the eighteenth century which had yielded so relatively painlessly to the upsurge of these business folk, they themselves in turn yielded no less painlessly to the upsurge of the working classes. It would be excessively innocent and naïve to be scandalized by the comparatively few examples of violent attempts to crush the extension of democracy in the mid nineteenth century. What is remarkable is the relative smoothness with which democratic ideas and institutions spread and grew within the hot-house atmosphere of the generation which built and admired the Crystal Palace.

CHAPTER VI

THE AGE OF PALMERSTON

Politics from Peel to Gladstone

SIR ROBERT PEEL's great ministry lasted from 1814 to 1846, and he was succeeded by Lord John Russell. Russell held power until 1852. From 1846 to 1874, when Disraeli formed his second ministry, the Whigs and Liberals dominated English government and were led at first by Russell, then by Palmerston, and finally by Gladstone. The Conservatives held office only for ten months under the Earl of Derby in 1852, for another sixteen months under Derby in 1858–9, for another two and a half years under Derby and Disraeli in 1866–8. It is noteworthy that the duration of Conservative governments tends to get steadily longer each time, but it is also noteworthy that they held office for less than five years altogether during the twenty-eight years between 1846 and 1874. What was the basis of this remarkable Liberal hegemony? First, the division between Liberals and Conservatives must be explained.

Gilbert and Sullivan suggested that the division was so much a part of the natural and accepted order of things

> That every boy and every gal
> That's born into this world alive,
> Is either a little Liberal,
> Or else a little Conserva-tive.

It was the practical counterpart to Macaulay's Whig interpretation of English history that such a two-party division should appear inherently natural. The ministry of Peel was in many respects the climax of the long period of Liberal-Tory administrations after 1815; in other respects it was the necessary adjustment of Toryism to the new middle-class ascendancy marked by the great Reform Bill and the other reorganizations of British administration and local government. It introduced a new element of confusion into party politics. Peel was accused of betraying his party over the repeal of the Corn Laws and his other free-trade measures, just as in 1829 he had 'betrayed' it over Catholic emancipation. In fact, after Peel's ministry, both parties accepted the broad principles of the Liberal creed and differed mainly over the speed and methods of their application. It thus became possible to have a real system of party-government, with parties alternating in power without each repealing the measures recently passed by its rival. Without this common ground the working of party-government would have been impossible. Socially it rested on the domination of both parties by the 'middle classes'. Economically it rested on the fact that, although there were great extremes of wealth and poverty, the gap between them was filled by the great extent of the middle classes.

The classical model of solid two-party government did not appear until the great duel between Gladstone and Disraeli after 1867. Between Peel's resignation in 1846 and the Second Reform Bill in 1867 there were nine administrations, several of which had no stable majority in Parliament.[1] Politics were dominated for most of that time by the most characteristically mid-Victorian statesman of all – Lord Palmerston (1784–1865); and by his policy of conservatism at home and jingoistic liberalism abroad he perpetuated great confusion among parties. He quarrelled with Russell, Aberdeen, and Gladstone, and was regarded as sufficiently non-party to be offered a place in Derby's Conservative administration of 1852. The truth was that he not only represented intuitively, but almost personally

1. See list of Ministries, p. 238.

embodied, the character and outlook of the commercial and industrial middle classes. So long as party discipline and organization were so loose, and party loyalties so confused, a figure like Palmerston was almost indispensable. He held office as Foreign Secretary under Lord Grey (1830–4), Lord Melbourne (1834 and 1835–41), Lord John Russell (1846–52); as Home Secretary under Lord Aberdeen (1852–5); and as Prime Minister (1855–8 and 1859–65). So there were only five years during this whole generation when Palmerston was not in power in an important office. It is, indeed, the age of Palmerston; and of Palmerston as the supreme personal spokesman of the hegemony of Liberalism. In the very ambiguity of his outlook and his position he perfectly represented the balance of social forces and the half-developed electoral system and parliamentary franchise of the mid-Victorian era. His political outlook and habits had been shaped in the years before the Reform Bill, and he carried over into the generation between the two Reform Bills the spirit of the pre-Reform Parliament. His death in 1865 is an important landmark in English political history. It released the more liberal forces in Liberalism from the restraints he had imposed, and was a necessary preliminary to the passing of a second Reform Bill in 1867. Only then could a sharper line of division appear between Conservatism and Liberalism – and only his foreign policy was continued by the new Conservative leader Disraeli. His death marks the end of an epoch.

The electoral system left by the Reform Bill of 1832 was the system whose workings were so well satirized by Dickens in *Pickwick Papers*. Eatanswill, if not characteristic of all mid-Victorian electioneering, was sufficiently vivid a satire on the tendencies of electioneering to bring ridicule upon them. The redistribution of seats, though remedying the worst of the old anomalies, had not been very thorough or systematic and was soon made out-of-date by the continued rapid growth of the big industrial towns. There were still boroughs sufficiently small in their electorate, and sufficiently unchanged in political traditions, to serve as pocket-boroughs for wealthy landlords and ambitious monied men. The Chandos clause, granting the vote to tenants-at-will in the counties, ensured that a large portion of the electorate should remain at the mercy of their landlords and subject to pressure at elections so long as there was no secret ballot. Because the Reform Bill made inclusion on the electoral register a technical qualification for any voter, party organizations concentrated on every device which – legitimate or not – might increase the number of their own supporters included on the register and diminish the number of their opponents. The restriction of times and places for polling led to more extensive and lavish efforts to make supporters merry enough to vote for you, and opponents drunk enough to be unable to vote at all. Elections consequently became often more disorderly than before, for larger numbers of voters were involved than before 1832. The 'semi-democratization' of the parliamentary system produced a form of political life which was unique in English history. It was a system which could not reflect any large and intelligent section of public opinion in our sense of the words, for popular elementary education and a cheap press had not yet advanced far enough to create such a thing. It did reflect the continued power of the landed and aristocratic classes, whilst making more room, in a somewhat crude and unsystematic way, for the wishes of the new industrial and commercial middle classes. For this reason the men returned to Parliament remained much the same sort of men (and often the very same men) in 1865 as in 1830. In 1833 there were 217 members of Parliament who were sons of peers or baronets; in 1860 there were 180, and even in 1880 there were 170. But the significance of this fact should not be exaggerated, for it became easier for men not of aristocratic parentage to reach very high political office. The elder Pitt had been exceptional in the eighteenth century, although even he had to marry into one of the Whig clans in order to get a solid footing in politics. Sir Robert Peel was the first son of a manufacturer to become Prime Minister; Lord Melbourne belonged to none of the aristocratic families, and his great-grandfather was an attorney; Gladstone belonged to a Scottish merchant-family of Liverpool; and Disraeli was the son of a Jewish literary man and grandson of a Jewish stockbroker. It is true that until after 1867 governments were led mostly by men of the old aristocracy – Grey, Russell, Derby, Palmerston – and only after 1867 did Gladstone, Disraeli, and more middle-class men come to predominate in cabinet office. But signs of the big change were already there in the time of Peel.

So long as most cabinet posts of importance were held by peers, two important consequences followed. One was that most members of the government had not been elected by any constituency, but sat in the Lords in their own right. The other was that debates in the House of Lords were every bit as important, politically, as debates in the House of Commons. The absence of at least half the members of the Government from the House of Commons and its debates meant that debates in the upper House were extremely important, and also that the power of the Prime Minister or his spokesman in the House of Commons was increased.

Although the number of constituencies actually contested in a general election after 1832 was much greater than during the eighteenth century, the chief effect of this, other than intensification of the bribery and disorder at election-time, was to promote the development of party organization for purposes of packing the electoral register. It did not lead to any extensive formation of local party organizations for purposes of propaganda and the formation of public opinion. The Carlton Club, founded in 1831, was concerned with organizing the registration of voters through local registration societies. The Conservative Central Office was not set up until 1852, and its chief function was to keep lists of approved candidates for elections. It also stimulated the formation of local associations. In 1867 the National Union of Conservative and Constitutional Associations was formed. Its aim was not so much to shape policy as to help to win elections. Meanwhile in 1835 the radicals had set up a registration office, and in 1838 founded the Reform Club to offset the Carlton Club. Typical party managers and agents of the time were Taper and Tadpole as Disraeli created them in *Coningsby* (1844).

> 'No repeal of any tax,' said Taper, sincerely shocked, and shaking his head; 'and the Malt Tax of all others. I am all against that.'
> 'It is a very good cry, though, if there be no other,' said Tadpole.
> 'I am all for a religious cry,' said Taper. 'It means nothing, and, if successful, does not interfere with business when we are in.'

The actual electorate, which had been increased by only some 50 per cent as the immediate consequence of 1832, had by 1866 come to include some 1,056,000 voters. This happened partly because of the total growth of population and partly because the rental qualifications, being fixed in monetary values, became wider as the value of money declined. But after the failure of Chartism in 1848 the more radical sections of public opinion became apathetic for a time. The demand for further reform of the electoral system and further extension of the franchise went on unheeded by Governments until the death of Palmerston, despite the efforts of men like John Bright to quicken that demand. Proletarian apathy is the counterpart to middle-class 'complacency' in the era of Palmerston: though the energies of the working class after the middle of the century were increasingly diverted into an ever-increasing number of trade unions and other labour organizations, which began to wield considerable power when mid-Victorian prosperity began to decline after 1870.

Broadly, the substance of Liberalism in home policy was still *laissez-faire* in economic life, involving low taxation, the piecemeal improvement of social conditions without radical overhaul, and the encouragement of private charity and voluntary association as the best remedies for surviving evils. Free trade was its main plank in commercial policy, peaceful international relations through expanding trade its foreign policy. Cobden's free-trade agreement with France in 1860 is perhaps the perfect specimen of what middle-class opinion most wanted its government to do in this period, although it was criticized by Palmerston on grounds of national security. It reduced French duties on coal and on most manufactured goods to rates not exceeding 30 per cent: in return Britain lowered duties on French wines and brandy. The value both of British exports to France and of French wines to England doubled between 1859 and 1869 as a result. Protectionism, the most obvious principle on which a reunited Conservative party might have been formed after the split caused by Peel in 1846, suffered real eclipse. Disraeli tried at first to do this, without success, and even Protectionists accepted an experiment in free trade as inevitable.

Throughout the Palmerstonian era foreign affairs dominated English politics much more than any single issue of domestic politics, and they will be more conveniently dealt with below (Chapter VIII). Otherwise, with free-trade principles so generally accepted at least for the time, the major domestic issue was taxation and finance. Gladstone, who was Chancellor of the Exchequer under Aberdeen

(1852–5), then under Palmerston (1859–65), framed his budgets on certain general principles which came to be regarded as the orthodox Liberal theory of national finance. He hoped to lower income tax by instalments and abolish it by 1859. He regarded it as 'an engine of gigantic power for great national purposes', and less a normal source of national revenue than an emergency expedient, as in time of war. He abolished most duties on partially manufactured goods and on food, and halved most duties on manufactured goods, so he had to find other sources of revenue. His chief hope was his extended legacy-duty. The military and naval expenditure involved in the Crimean War and the suppression of the Indian Mutiny, combined with the other international tensions of these years, led to the increasing of income tax to 1s 2d in 1854, and its retention after the war at 9d until 1863, when he reduced it to 7d. By 1865 it was down to 4d and the duties on tea and sugar were also greatly reduced. The biggest reform which Gladstone effected in the fiscal system was the reduction of the number of varying import duties. His Budget of 1860 reduced them from 419 to 48, at a loss to the revenue of only one million pounds. He also abolished the paper duty in the interests of a cheap press, despite opposition from Palmerston. Such thorough-going simplification of the fiscal system marks the end of the old financial order and the beginning of the new.

The Second Reform Bill

The major political issue of the sixties concerned the next step in the process of parliamentary reform. Few Englishmen now regarded the arrangements of 1832 as a final settlement, but there was wide disagreement, cutting across all parties, as to how and when the parliamentary franchise and the electoral system should be further altered. There was no logic or consistency in a system which prescribed three different kinds of franchise – one for election of poor-law Guardians, one for local elections, and one for parliamentary elections. When so much social legislation had been passed promoting the public health, better working conditions, and general welfare of the working classes, it began to seem illogical that so much should be done for the workers without granting them some share in deciding and shaping the measures. In 1852, and again in 1854, Lord John Russell brought in mild and tepid reform bills, but both were killed. They were too early. After the commotion caused by the Crimean War John Bright began an intensive campaign to stir the workers to demand further reform. In 1859 Disraeli brought in a complicated proposal of reform which crashed the Derby government. The next year Russell tried again and failed. Other proposals in 1861 and 1864 were rejected, mainly as a result of opposition from Palmerston. Gladstone sponsored the cause, declaring that 'every man who is not presumably incapacitated . . . is morally entitled to come within the pale of the Constitution.' When, in 1865, Palmerston died and John Bright renewed his campaign with increased vigour, the idea found at last a positive public response. For some fifteen years men of all parties had come out in favour of reform and the need for it was becoming very apparent. Yet when, in 1866, Russell and Gladstone proposed a very moderate extension of the vote to some 400,000 people it brought down Russell's government. It was left, paradoxically, to his Conservative successor, Disraeli, as the strongest man in Derby's third cabinet, to bring in the bill which eventually became law: and in the process of becoming law it became, equally paradoxically, a much more radical measure of reform than even Disraeli wanted.

The Conservatives' sponsoring of the Bill was an item

of party strategy. A reform bill had become inevitable. The pressure of public agitation ensured that. Better, then, a bill framed by Conservatives who would reap the double benefit of ensuring its moderation and claiming the credit. The ministry was divided over the details of the proposal. It was agreed that household suffrage should be the basis, but most ministers wanted some safeguards such as plural voting or rating qualifications. Disraeli wanted primarily a durable settlement and was prepared to go a good way to get it. The draft proposals were hurriedly prepared one week-end, and some ministers found them so radical that they resigned. Under pressure from Gladstone and the Liberal and Radical opposition the bill in its passing became still more radical because the safeguards were mostly dropped. In the event the vote in the counties went to all occupiers of houses rated at £12 or more and all leaseholders with property of at least £4 annual value; in the boroughs, to all householders who had been in residence for at least one year and lodgers paying £10 or more per annum. Some forty-five seats were redistributed so as to strengthen the representation of the counties and the larger towns at the expense of the smaller towns. The effect was to increase the middle-class vote in the counties and extend the vote to the artisans and better-to-do workers in the towns, although the smaller boroughs were still over-represented in the Commons. As after 1832, the new voters tended to return the same sort of men as had sat in Parliament before 1867. Now, even more certainly than after 1832, a still further instalment of parliamentary reform was inevitable. Parliament was subject to new electoral pressures. There was nothing sacrosanct about the sharp and invidious distinction made by the Act between workers in town and country. And – most significant of the new urban England which had come into existence – for the first time in English history the boroughs had more voters than the counties. Even so, the whole electorate was less than a tenth of the total population.

The political consequences of the Act were, however, much greater than the purely electoral changes. Bigger constituencies and bigger electorates called for much more elaborate party organization; for the Act had nearly doubled the number of people who had a vote. The House of Lords had introduced an amendment which stipulated that in the few big towns, Liverpool, Manchester, Birmingham, and Leeds, now entitled to return three members to Parliament, no elector should vote for more than two of the candidates. The aim was to ensure the representation of minorities. The Birmingham Liberal Association soon discovered that by careful distribution of their voting-strength they could capture all three seats for their party, but to achieve this they had to organize their supporters with great care. This led to the formation of the Birmingham Liberal 'caucus', which did its job so well that its methods were retained, improved, and imitated, providing a great new stimulus to the integration of party organization. The freedom both of members and of local committees was restricted in favour of party discipline and the power of the central organization. In 1867 the National Union of Conservative and Constitutional Associations was formed, and ten years later the National Federation of Liberal Associations. What Sir John Gorst did for the Conservatives, Schnadhorst did for the Liberals, and both parties by the 1880s had assumed their more modern highly centralized structure.

Local government franchise was brought into line with parliamentary franchise in the boroughs, for the Act of 1867 was made to apply to municipal elections as well as to parliamentary. In 1868 separate Reform Bills were passed

for Scotland and Ireland, bringing those countries roughly
into line with England and giving Scotland seven additional
members. Even relations between the two Houses of Parliament were altered by the Act, because it sharpened the
difference between the political bases of the two Houses: the
more democratic and representative became the Commons,
the more distinctly it emphasized the aristocratic character
of the Lords. Future conflict between them became more
and more likely. But voting still remained public, not
secret, and although Ballot Committees and Ballot Societies
had been active since 1832 the Liberal Party was committed
to secret ballot only after 1870 and passed it only at the
third attempt in 1872. So obvious a protection for the
working-class or even middle-class voter against unjust
pressure and victimization seems to us a natural corollary to
the extension of the vote. No more illuminating insight into
the political mind of the mid-Victorians is offered than a
study of the arguments produced against secret ballot. Even
so lucid and progressive a mind as Sydney Smith's had
failed to see that there was nothing sinister or undemocratic
in privacy of voting. He argued that open voting was more
dignified than the secretive protection of men who, if they
had not courage enough to proclaim their vote publicly,
were not fit to vote at all: and that men with the courage of
their convictions should not be forced to vote secretly to
save the face of cowards. Yet Eatanswill was the result of
open voting.

The Apparatus of the New State

By 1870 it was clear that if the British State was to fulfil
efficiently the many new tasks it had undertaken it needed
thorough overhaul and reorganization. A long series of
reforms culminated in the concentrated 'political engineer-

ing' achievements of Gladstone's First Ministry (1868–74). In those years the basis of the modern State was well and truly laid. So much could be achieved in so short a time only because the ground had been already prepared, there was steady pressure for reform from public opinion in the country, and many reforms had already been so long delayed that they were accepted as overdue and now inevitable. Three main branches of government – the civil service, the military organization, and the judiciary – were overhauled within a few years.

In 1853 Macaulay had reformed the Indian Civil Service by substituting for the older system of recruitment by patronage and influence a system of recruitment by competitive examination in tests of high academic standard. In the same year a strong Commission on the organization of the permanent civil service recommended its division into two classes consisting of men between 19 and 25 enrolled for intellectual work and men between 17 and 19 for mechanical work. They suggested open competitive examination as the proper way of recruiting both classes, but wanted promotion from one class to the other to be very rare. Although these recommendations met with fierce opposition from many sides, in 1855 three Civil Service Commissioners were appointed to hold such competitive examinations. At first each Department kept its own tests and the system worked badly, until an Order in Council of 1870 abolished patronage and made competitive examinations compulsory. It also introduced the two-grade system which persists to-day. As the State could not perform the many labours of social service organization which it was assuming until its own machinery was improved these reforms were the very basis of further change.

As in the civil administration, so in the military, the old system rested on patronage and influence, and it was greatly discredited by the blunders and breakdowns of the Army in the Crimean War. The old evils were many and affected every level of the Army: the division of responsibility between the Commander-in-Chief appointed by the Crown and the Secretary of State for War and Colonies; the placing of the Militia, Yeomanry, and Volunteers under the Home Office and not the Secretary of State for War; the system of purchasing commissions and promotion in the Army, except in the Artillery and the Engineers; the miserable and brutalizing conditions of service among lower ranks. Any change in the system was bitterly resisted by the Duke of Wellington and the old guard, and as late as 1871 even Lord John Russell justified purchase of commissions. The rapid victories of Prussia in the sixties and the crisis of the Franco-Prussian War in 1870 focused attention on the Army and prompted its speedy overhaul. Edward Cardwell, Gladstone's Secretary of State for War, did for military reforms what Chadwick and Trevelyan did for civil service reform. He abolished flogging in the Army in peace-time and got rid of some of its worst characters. In 1870 he abolished purchase of commissions, using royal warrant to do it when his Army Regulation Bill including the change was shelved by the House of Lords. He made the Commander-in-Chief subordinate to the Secretary of State for War, thereby restricting royal power and ensuring unity of direction. All land forces without exception were placed under the Commander-in-Chief, thereby depriving the landed gentry who served as Lords-Lieutenant of their power to appoint officers in the Militia. He raised the quality of recruiting by replacing the old system of long-term service by a system of six years' enlistment and six years on the reserve list, but low pay and unattractive conditions still hampered recruitment. He reorganized equipment and the regimental groupings of the infantry, but

failed to reorganize the cavalry and artillery. All these reforms, regarded as a major attack on the most deeply entrenched oligarchic interests, had to be forced through by
any device available against bitter opposition. The result
was a military force capable of later adaptation and expansion to face the ordeal of 1914.

Lord Selborne, Gladstone's Lord Chancellor between
1872 and 1874, did for the judiciary what Cardwell did for
the Army. He simplified and remodelled both the legal
system and the courts which administered it. He fused the
systems of common law and equity, henceforth to be administered concurrently in all courts. He took the seven old
courts of common law – the King's Bench, Common Pleas,
Exchequer, Chancery, Admiralty, Probate, and Divorce,
and unified them within one Supreme Court of Judicature,
divided into the Court of Appeal and the High Court of
Justice. By 1880 the present threefold division was established: King's Bench, Chancery, and Probate, Divorce
and Admiralty, and any judge of the High Court could sit
in any division. His attempt to replace the House of Lords
by the Court of Appeal failed. Again one of the most conservative and traditional branches of government was taken
out into the light, dusted and reshaped, and made fitter for
its contemporary duties.

These reforms, coming so soon after the widening of the
franchise in 1867 and preceding the increase in State and
municipal activities in the last quarter of the century, offer
some insight into the whole development of English government. They are the counterpart to the great adjustments of
political and economic machinery which followed the first
Reform Bill and are in part the further consequences of
those earlier adjustments. Throughout the century between
1815 and 1914 there was constant interplay between the
development of social-welfare legislation and the progress of

parliamentary reform. Social betterment made further extension of the franchise possible and more probable, and extensions of the franchise led to fresh programmes of social improvement. The two best examples of this interplay concern public health legislation and education.

The great interest in improvement of public health between 1848 and 1874 sprang from two very dynamic forces – the cholera and Edwin Chadwick. In 1838 Chadwick got a board of doctors to enquire into the causes of destitution and death, first in London and then in the rest of the country. Their report led Parliament to set up a commission of enquiry into town life, and its report of 1846 led to Chadwick's legislation of 1848. The report showed that the gross inadequacy of water supplies, drainage, and facilities for the disposal of refuse in the big towns were the biggest sources of disease. The return of the dreaded cholera in 1848 drew public attention to the urgency of the problem. A central board of health was created on the lines of the Poor Law Commissioners. It had certain powers to create local boards. It was abolished in 1858, but in 1865–6 a further outbreak of cholera forced the issue. Local authorities were now compelled to appoint sanitary inspectors and to undertake the provision of sewers, water supply, and refuse disposal. In 1869 a further commission drew up a statement of the basic conditions 'necessary for civilized social life' – the germ of the later idea of a basic subsistence-level and a minimum standard of living. The Local Government Board was set up to supervise all such work, including the Poor Law. In 1919 it became the present Ministry of Health. All this activity and provision was on behalf of the town workers; but until 1867 none of it could come from direct pressure from them through Parliament, though some pressure was directed through the municipal franchise. When the central authority was assuming so much power and doing so many more positive things affecting intimately the welfare of all, it became increasingly absurd to deny the beneficiaries some say in parliamentary elections and the general decisions of national policy.

Similarly in education there was little progress towards a national system of public education before 1867. There were plenty of schools, but no general system. In 1833 the first grant of public money (£20,000) was made for the building of schools. A commission of 1858 recommended the setting up of local Education Boards. It was the Reform Bill of 1867 which gave the first real impetus to the creation of a national system of free and compulsory education, and in 1869 the National Education League was founded at Birmingham by the radicals. The Education Act of 1870 set up locally-elected school boards which could compel attendance to the age of thirteen. Fees could be remitted for poor parents. It all followed the familiar pattern of poor law and public health reforms: commissions of enquiry, followed by public pressure from the new electorate and by parliamentary legislation setting up locally elected boards and a means test. Only in 1918 were school fees abolished in all elementary schools. The more rapid growth of popular education had been prevented partly by the clash between Church and Dissent, partly by the apathy of the people.

Again, a wider franchise demanded a better educated electorate, and at the same time facilitated provision for educating the people. This, in turn, made still further extensions of the franchise feasible. Always this interplay between political and social change produced a similar result: an increase in both central and local governmental activity and in central authority and responsibility; an increase in the number of State employees, whether inspectors, civil servants, or teachers. A quite new kind of State was quickly coming into existence. It has since come to be known as the social-service State, and is now the common pattern of political and social life in the twentieth century. Great developments have since taken place for the same reasons which operated in the mid-Victorian era. Because the State was being step by step democratized, new social classes claimed benefits from the State and laid claim to use the State for their own ends. Therefore the State had to adjust, extend, and develop its machinery to serve new ends of social control and public service. This meant considerable changes in the nature and functioning of Parliament. On the other hand, because the State undertook more and more tasks, interfered more in private life, and was being equipped with greater and more efficient sources of power, it had to be more and more democratized. Personal liberty was felt to be more and more endangered, so safeguards for popular freedoms and rights had to be strengthened. This meant more perfect electoral machinery, a more active and better informed public opinion, more scope for voluntary societies. On the whole the Radicals, and later the Socialists, urged the former argument, the Liberals urged the latter. Because both were in constant interplay during the formative decades of the seventies and eighties, Liberalism was socialized and Socialism was liberalized, unlike their counterparts on the continent of Europe. There grew up a strong tradition of 'Liberal Socialism' which was completely within the traditions and institutions of parliamentary government, and which made possible that alliance between Liberals and Socialists which was the mainspring of domestic politics in the decade before 1914. But to this we shall return later.[1] Meanwhile, further light is thrown on this whole tendency by closer examination of the radical and labour movements during the years between 1848 and 1874.

1. Chapter X below.

CHAPTER VII

THE AGE OF MACHINERY

Changes in Economic Organization

THE population of England and Wales increased by some five millions between 1851 and 1871. This increase was due to all three causes which can increase population: immigration, higher birth-rate, and lower death-rate. During these twenty years the birth-rate rose from 33.9 per 1000 to 35.3 per 1000: the death-rate fell from 22.7 per 1000 to 22.4 per 1000. Immigrants still came mostly from Ireland and Scotland, but some 3,700,000 emigrants left the United Kingdom for America during these years.

How did the 21 million inhabitants of the United Kingdom mainly find their living? Agriculture was still Britain's largest national industry. It employed some 1,790,000 people. Next to it came textiles, employing more than 1,650,000 in 1851. The growth and wealth of the middle classes are reflected in the fact that over a million people were engaged as domestic servants. The heavy industries were growing fast. By 1871 more than three-quarters of a million were employed in metal, engineering, and ship-building trades. The development of machinery meant that 106,000 were engaged in making machines. Half a million more were engaged in mines and quarries. The mileage of railroads doubled between these dates, and the big railway companies arose from amalgamations of smaller ones. They employed over 65,000 people in 1851. Modern Britain, industrialized, mechanized, and urbanized, was coming into being. Already suburbanism, at least around London, had begun: and more than 3,254,000 people lived in the capital, constituting a city of unprecedented size.

This was the period when Britain enjoyed to the full the economic benefits of having become the 'workshop of the world'. Her total exports in 1850 were worth £71,000,000, in 1870 they were worth nearly £200,000,000. Her imports trebled in these years from £100,000,000 to £300,000,000. The gap between imports and exports was more than bridged by her 'invisible exports' in the form of shipping, banking, and insurance services. Her revenue rose from £57,576,000 to £75,434,000. Deposits in the savings banks rose from £30,000,000 to £53,000,000. The Post Office Savings Bank was established in 1861, and by the early seventies was handling accounts totalling £18,000,000. Whichever way it is looked at, the total wealth of the country was growing fast, and it was more widely distributed throughout the community than before. Better wages, improvements in conditions in the mines, factories, and towns, and regulation of hours of work, as well as the growth of free social services such as public health and education, meant that the poor were much better off at the end of the period than they had been twenty years before. Workers in most of the textile industries had a working day of 10½ hours and a 60-hour week with holidays on Saturday afternoons. The greatest abuses in the employment of women and children had been removed. Though the workers' lot was still harsh by modern standards, it was very much better than a generation earlier. Progressive extensions in 1860, 1864, and 1867 of the legal definitions of what constituted a 'factory' gave wider protection to industrial workers under the Factory Acts. With the improvement in recruitment and organization of the civil service, already noted, the State was able more confidently and effectively to regulate conditions of labour. Pressure from labour organizations and the electorate ensured that it should continue to do so.

The years of Gladstone's First Ministry were marked by a big boom in trade. There was an almost universal inflation of credit and business as well as of prices. The demand for railways and ships abroad underlay the boom in iron, steel, and coal. The price of cotton remained high after the American Civil War (1860–5). Money wages rose sharply between 1870 and 1873. Since the price of food rose very little a larger part of the wage-packet was available to be spent on other things, or to be saved. The consumption of tea, sugar, and such commodities increased. Trade union funds swelled, constituting a form of small savings, for they were drawn from the weekly contributions of their members. It is significant of the whole history of Victorian England that the climax of its material prosperity meant also the strengthening of labour organizations which were to play so large a part in the criticism and transformation of its principles of free enterprise and competitive capitalism. As usual, it bred its own critics, and in every respect it was the seed-bed of the twentieth century.

Meanwhile the structure of capitalism itself was changing. Old family firms tended to be replaced by limited liability companies run by salaried managers. As Professor Trevelyan has put it,

> The 'shareholder' as such had no knowledge of the lives, thoughts, or needs of the workmen employed by the Company in which he held shares, and his influence on the relations of capital and labour was not good. The paid manager acting for the company was in more direct relation with the men and their demands, but even he had seldom that familiar personal knowledge of the workmen which the employer had often had under the patriarchal system of the old family business now passing away. (*Social History*, p. 573.)

The units of production being larger, workshops and factories were tending to get larger. In 1871 the average cotton factory employed 180 people, the average hosiery factory 71 people. The average in iron shipbuilding (78 firms) was 570: in iron-works, 209. Limited liability companies were made possible by legislation of 1855–6. Concentration of capital and encouragement of larger undertakings were promoted by the Companies Act of 1862, satirized by W. S. Gilbert:

> Some seven men form an Association
> (If possible, all Peers and Baronets)
> They start off with a public declaration
> To what extent they mean to pay their debts.
> That's called their Capital.

Provided their object was lawful, any seven men could become a company, with limited or unlimited liability, merely by subscribing a memorandum of association. Between 1880 and 1885 about 560 private firms were converted into companies, but before 1880 the conversion of old businesses was slow. More remarkable was the rapid development of joint stock companies during the sixties. In 1864, for example, 975 new companies were registered with a nominal capital of £235,000,000; and in the following year 1014 were registered, with a 'capital' of £203,000,000. The annual crop of registrations remained of this order throughout the seventies, and by 1887 it was twice as large: but it must be remembered that only some 10 per cent of the nominal capital of new companies registered was paid up in cash. The accumulated new wealth of Britain was poured by these means into capitalist enterprise, both at home and overseas.

The centre of control of both the national and international financial systems lay in the City of London. Sterling, anchored to the gold standard by Peel's Bank Act of 1844, became the money of international finance. Professor E. H. Carr has summed it up thus:

> The corollary of an international commodity market was an international discount market, an international market for shipping

freights, an international insurance market, and, finally, an international capital market. (*Nationalism and After*, p. 14.)

Sterling provided an international monetary standard into which separate national currencies were exchangeable at fixed rates: and the custodian of the standard of sterling was the London money market, ultimately controlled by the Bank of England. When that astute banker, Walter Bagehot, in 1873 wrote his study of *Lombard Street*, he remarked that 'Money will not manage itself, and Lombard Street has a great deal of money to manage.' As he pointed out, London after the eclipse of Paris in 1870 became 'the sole great settling-house of exchange transactions in Europe, instead of being formerly one of two.' This gave the City a sort of constant control over the money of the world, and meant that the world economic order, which was regarded by *laissez-faire* economists as part of the natural order, was in fact controlled by a highly centralized authority situated in London. It was, as Bagehot suggested, an odd kind of authority:

> The result is that we have placed the exclusive custody of our entire banking reserve in the hands of a single board of directors not particularly trained for the duty – who might be called 'amateurs' – who have no particular interest above other people in keeping it undiminished – who acknowledge no obligation to keep it undiminished – who have never been told by any great statesman or public authority that they are so to keep it or that they have anything to do with it – who are named by and are agents for a proprietary which would have a greater income if it was diminished – who do not fear, and who need not fear, ruin, even if it were all gone and wasted. (*Lombard Street*, p. 44.)

Backed by the stability of the London money market and the silent but constant security provided by the Navy, Britain's overseas traffic multiplied more than four times in bulk between 1847 and 1880: for the tonnage of shipping entered and cleared from British ports, excluding coastal and Anglo-Irish trade, was 14,300,000 in 1847, and 58,700,000 in 1880. Apart from the set-back after 1847 there had been a steady increase throughout this period of between 50 and 60 per cent each decade. At the time of the Great Exhibition more than half the world's ocean-going tonnage of shipping was British. This supremacy seemed like declining during the second half of the century, as United States overseas trade developed; but the American Civil War and American concentration on western expansion left Britain with a greater share of the traffic of the high seas for the rest of the century than she enjoyed at any other time in her whole history. The opening of the Suez Canal in 1869 brought Britain great advantages. Of the 2,263,300 tons of shipping that passed through it in 1879, 1,752,400 tons were British. It had been built with French capital, but in 1874 Disraeli bought the Egyptian Khedive's shares and gained for Britain a large share of control. After it had been widened and improved in the eighties, more than three-quarters of the shipping using it was British.

The rapid development of industry, dependent upon imports for much of its raw materials other than coal and iron, combined with the growth of population and of overseas trade, meant that the country was becoming increasingly dependent on imports for its food supplies as well. Although the full extent of this development belongs to the twentieth century, already by 1880 nearly three-quarters of the corn Britain consumed came from overseas. In all these ways Britain was ceasing to be an island.

Nor was it shipping and trade alone that linked the British Isles to the rest of the world and bound their fate so closely to what might be happening in any part of the globe. In the sixties the technical problems of laying deep-sea cables were solved, after twenty years of experiments and disappointments. Thousands of miles of cable had been laid, but by 1861 only 3000 miles of it were working. In that year the United Kingdom Telegraph Company was formed, to experiment with the novelty of a uniform rate within the United Kingdom irrespective of distance. At last in 1870, after a period of hesitation and of wasteful competition between rival telegraph companies, the telegraph system was bought up by the Post Office. By 1885 it was able to introduce the sixpenny telegram. During the seventies this national system became linked more and more closely with other countries by the deep-sea cables. In 1870 there was a direct cable from London to Bombay; in 1874, South America was linked to Europe. By the eighties the whole world, save the most remote corners such as Honolulu, New Guinea, and the heart of China, was reduced for economic purposes to one market, and communication no longer depended on distance.

These immense changes in the structure of economic and social life called for great adjustments in both the habits of thought and the forms of labour organization of the new generation of English people. The basic fact was improvement in the standard of living. If in more recent times such improvement can be largely attributed to the action of labour organizations, in this period it is truer to attribute the rise of successful labour organizations to the improvement of conditions. Money wages, with a few slight lapses, rose steadily between 1850 and 1874. From a base of 100 in 1850 it has been calculated that the general level rose to 156 by 1874, and even by 1886 had not dropped lower than 148. Prices, on the other hand, rose sharply between 1848 and 1854, and again between 1870 and 1873; and after 1873, although wages fell, prices fell even faster during the two big slumps. For these reasons the standard of living and prosperity of the mass of the workers rose greatly throughout the period. Professor Clapham has given a warning about these statistical calculations which it is important to remember:

> A man who had worked at the same trade from the Great Exhibition to the eve of Victoria's Jubilee, without losing any of his efficiency, could not show a rise of 48 per cent in his weekly wage like this 'average wage-earner'; though one who had left the land as a young man for some urban job might show more. The man who had remained in the station of life in which he was born had, on the average, lived to see a rise in his weekly or hourly rate of pay of something like 30 per cent. About this figure different trades and jobs fluctuated. (*Economic History of Modern Britain*, Vol. II, p. 451.)

This all meant that in 1870 most working-class families were absolutely better off by about ten per cent than they had been in 1850. It was on the firm basis of such prosperity that trade unionism, the cooperative movement, and other labour organizations grew and thrived. The result was a variety of 'Liberal Socialism' which may now be more closely examined.

The Birth of Liberal Socialism

Most of the reforms described in the previous chapter were put through Parliament by Liberals and Radicals, with some pressure from outside Parliament generated by radical and labour agitation in the country. Some – such as the Reform Bill of 1867 itself – were directly the result of the competitive party-system, wherein Liberals and Conservatives rivalled each other in winning votes by making concessions to the more progressive sections of public opinion. But they were only in the most indirect and imperfect way the achievements of organized workmen. Chartism had been quelled in 1848, and in the fifties working men sank into a decade of comparative apathy and inertia in politics. Chartism had been basically the product of hunger and distress and it died when the growth of British trade improved wages and the standard of living, governmental repressiveness slackened, and unemployment became less prevalent. Although much real distress continued among less skilled workers, the more skilled were enjoying better times and this destroyed the chance of a mass-movement based on economic distress. The more skilled were turning, however, to new methods of organization such as trade unionism and the cooperative movement, and these great changes brought a vital revolution in the whole character of labour organization in England.

Trade unionism, so far as its internal structure was concerned, had almost to begin again in the fifties. The old 'General Unions' of Owen, John Doherty, and the pioneers of the thirties had been smashed by 1835. They had grown too fast to have any solid strength. In the forties new and more small-scale unions grew up gradually among the more skilled workers of the heavy industries. The Miners' Association was formed in 1841, and many separate engineering unions appeared. In 1845 was formed the National Association of United Trades for the Protection of Labour, and in 1851 the famous Amalgamated Society of Engineers, with some 11,000 members including nearly all the engineering unions. Thus the new unions, based on particular kinds of skilled industrial labour, grew up on a firmer basis than the old. They were stronger financially and more open in their discussions and activity. They were still, like their predecessors, hampered by legal restrictions and prohibitions, but they were not driven into behaving like secret societies. Insurance and social benefits were a large part of their work, as well as collective bargaining with employers. An embryonic trades union congress met in Manchester in 1868, and represented some 118,000 trade unionists. In the early seventies the unions were greater legal protection, both for their own internal funds and organization, and for their favourite methods of collective bargaining and peaceful picketing. When Gladstone formed his First Ministry trade unionism was an accepted and well-established feature of English industrial life. That its growth was relatively so smooth and peaceful was largely due to the victories won by the defunct unions of the days of Owen, and to the repeal of the Combination Laws in 1824–5. They could now grow in step with the development of industrialization, as part of it and of English life.

It is characteristic of the traditions and spirit of this new unionism that its first impulse was to get representatives into Parliament. It was radical and democratic in character, not Marxist, and it remains one of the remarkable facts of English history that although Marx and Engels lived and worked in England throughout the formative decades of the labour movement they exercised virtually no influence at all on its development. The London Working Men's Association was formed in 1866, and in the year of the Second Reform Bill it organized the London trade unions in support of the Bill. Its aim, once the Bill was passed, was to promote the election of working men to Parliament, and to assert trade-union interests which were to come under consideration in the new Parliament. It did not aim to form a distinct Labour Party, but to return independents who could collaborate with Radicals and Liberals as individual Radicals had done in the recent past. There was not yet in any sense a Socialist movement in England. Their demands were for manhood suffrage, a juster redistribution of seats, secret ballot, reform of the land law, a national system of education, legal protection of trade union rights, and legislation to improve housing and factory conditions. It was a labour movement and it wanted social reforms as well as political reforms: but it was not a Socialist movement, wanting a basic change in the economic system, and it was not a revolutionary movement.

The London Working Men's Association broke new ground but it did not build on the new ground. By 1870 it had ceased to count in national politics, and was replaced by the Labour Representation League, composed of Radical, Socialist, and trade union groups in London. This defined its aims as twofold:

> The League will promote throughout the kingdom the registration of working-men's votes without reference to their opinions or party bias; its aim being to organize fully the strength of the operative classes as an electoral power . . .
>
> Its principal duty will be to secure the return to Parliament of qualified working men – persons who, by character and ability, command the confidence of their class . . .

Springing from the contacts established in the capital between Radicals and trade union organizers, it began as a predominantly London body. It planned the formation of local branches throughout the country, but never succeeded in doing more than collaborating with local workers' Radical associations based on individual membership rather than on organized labour. It did not, therefore, become very powerful. It achieved little beyond rousing working-class opinion to take an interest in parliamentary and municipal elections.

It was at the third attempt to get working-class spokesmen into Parliament that a real political labour movement was to grow. This rested on the Parliamentary Committee of the new Trades Union Congress, set up in 1869. It found its main task in organizing opposition to certain of the results of Gladstone's Criminal Law Amendment Act of 1871. His Trade Union Act of the same year gave protection to trade union funds and strengthened the legal status of labour unions generally. But the Criminal Law Amendment Act, which had originally been a part of the Trade Union Bill, took away some of the apparent protection given by the other Act. It defined molestation, obstruction, and intimidation as criminal offences so widely as to make any strike action extremely dangerous for trade unionists. Taken together the two Acts meant Liberal recognition of the unions as friendly and benefit societies and as vehicles of peaceful collective bargaining, but severe restriction of their powers as fighting bodies. This restriction provoked the unions to strong and solid protest and gave them a clear political purpose which they had so far lacked.

Between 1871 and 1875 political agitation coincided with pressure for better working conditions exerted through direct action. 'The years from 1871 onwards,' writes Mr G. D. H. Cole, 'were fuller of strikes than any period since the collapse of the Grand National Consolidated Trades Union in 1834.' Miners, engineers, shipbuilders, builders, and agricultural workers took advantage of the industrial boom of the early seventies to press for greater advantages in wages and hours of work. The series of strikes and lock-outs after 1875 were mainly efforts to resist reductions in wages, and many of them failed. The great depression of 1879, brought a new and more desperate phase in trade unionism, wherein unemployment was its greatest weakness.

This increasing concentration on economic problems diverted energy from the political struggle. Such benefits as the working classes had gained by 1880 were derived hardly at all from their direct representation in Parliament, and almost entirely from direct bargaining or from the competition between Liberals and Conservatives for their electoral support. In the elections of 1874 thirteen working-class or Labour candidates stood, but only two – who were miners – got in. In 1875 Disraeli tried to capture union support by repealing the Criminal Law Amendment Act,

and the Conspiracy and Protection of Property Act with
which he replaced it restored the right of peaceful picketing
and otherwise narrowed the legal definitions of molestation,
obstruction, and intimidation. The further Employers and
Workmen Act gave workers greater equality before the law,
and the Trade Union Amendment Act of 1876 rounded off
the legal rights of trade unions in favour of the unions. These
concessions destroyed the impetus behind the Labour
Representation League. The trade unions turned again to
support of the Liberals (with whom their strong nonconformist tendencies formed a powerful social link) now that
old controvesies between them had been removed by the
Conservatives, and by 1880 the League had practically
withered away.

The close connexion between labour and trade union
movements, and Radical and Liberal political movements,
which is thus the most outstanding feature of the formative
period of trade union organization between 1850 and 1880,
laid the basis for that growth of Liberal Socialism which is
the special characteristic of modern Britain. On one hand
Radical, Liberal, and even Conservative parties were
brought into close contact with labour movements and made
familiar with the needs of the working classes. On the other,
labour and Socialist movements turned recurrently and per-
sistently to political and parliamentary methods of action.
Direct action was never regarded as a satisfactory sub-
stitute for parliamentary action. Social democracy was
something of a practical reality in English life before the
more doctrinaire movements which assumed that label
made their appearance in the eighties.

These facts were of momentous importance for the future
of both Socialism and democracy in modern Britain.
Syndicalism in its European pattern gained no hold in
Britain, because for two generations the growth of trade

unionism and the growth of parliamentary Liberalism and Radicalism were inextricably mixed. Though the gains of unionism were slow, they were positive and permanent, and labour demands upon Parliament did not meet with stubborn refusals. On the other hand, the aim of securing direct labour representation in Parliament had not yet been fulfilled: and that ambition remained deep within the spirit of trade unionism. It was satisfied, as will be shown later, by similar cooperation with political and parliamentary movements reared in the common soil of democratic idealism.

Simultaneously another form of working-class movement had been making enormous strides. This was the Cooperative movement, founded in 1844 when a group of twenty-eight Lancashire working men opened a little store in Toad Lane, Rochdale. Six of them were Chartists, six Owenites, and most of them trade unionists. It was the most solid and impressively successful piece of working-class self-help which emerged from the many experiments of the period. The scheme of distributing dividends to registered members of the society kept it extremely democratic in shape. By 1851 there were some 130 Cooperative stores in the north of England and in Scotland. Within twenty years their methods spread to wholesale trading as well as retail, and to production as well as to distribution. The Cooperative Wholesale Society was formed in Manchester in 1864, and by 1886 its profits exceeded £20,000. Total membership of the English societies rose to 250,000 by 1871 and to 805,000 by 1889. The Cooperative movement, a characteristic product of this age, had even more direct links with the ideas of Robert Owen than has modern trade unionism. Its sturdy self-reliant spirit had a great appeal to the thrifty working-class housewives, especially in the north and in Scotland.

These gropings in the sixties for new forms of self-help and self-improvement, including new forms of social organization, coincided with a profound change of mood and mental outlook in the younger generation of the sixties and seventies. Mr E. R. Pease, the historian of the Fabian Society, has expressed it like this:

> It is nowadays not easy to recollect how wide was the intellectual gulf which separated the young generation of that period from their parents. *The Origin of Species*, published in 1859, inaugurated an intellectual revolution such as the world had not known since Luther nailed his theses to the door of All Saints Church at Wittenberg. The older folk as a rule refused to accept or to consider the new doctrine. I recollect a botanical Fellow of the Royal Society who, in 1875, told me that he had no opinions on Darwin's hypothesis. The young men of the time grew up with the new ideas and accepted them as a matter of course . . . Our parents, who read neither Spencer nor Huxley, lived in an intellectual world which bore no relation to our own; and cut adrift as we were from the intellectual moorings of our upbringings, recognizing, as we did, that the older men were useless as guides in religion, in science, in philosophy, because they knew no evolution, we also felt instinctively that we could accept nothing on trust from those who still believed that the early chapters of Genesis accurately described the origin of the universe, and that we had to discover somewhere for ourselves what were the true principles of the then recently invented science of sociology.

This stirring of 'Liberal Socialism' came fully to the surface in the eighties and nineties, and gave birth to the new Labour Party.

In these ways the enormous increase in the population, wealth, and power of mid-Victorian England carried with it important changes in methods of economic organization and in forms of labour organization. The age of machinery was also the age of organization: and industrial relations became more impersonal, less a matter of human relationships between man and man than social relationships between one large organization and another. This new impersonality of economic relations brought with it new social tensions. On one hand men and women had to get used to being more 'organized' than they had ever been before, and this called for often painful adjustments of old ways of life and thought. Their habits, conditions of work, and even their wages were determined more for them by the interaction of big associations or by governmental regulation. On the other, a new stratum of middlemen had come between the mass of the workers and the owners of factory, mine, or mill: a class of managers and foremen, or of trade union organizers and government inspectors. What mattered now was the relationship of the worker to organizers and organizations, rather than his relationship to his employer. Although in the long run these changes meant greater security, improved conditions, and higher wages, in the short run they brought problems of human adjustment which were seldom solved without distress. The distress was, however, alleviated by the growing prosperity and by the Liberal spirit which prevailed during this middle generation. The worst phase of sweating and of severe hardship was over before 1850.

CHAPTER VIII

THE AGE OF PRESTIGE AND EXPANSION

The Policy of Prestige

MENTION has already been made (Chapter VI) of the almost symbolic role of Lord Palmerston in British foreign policy. The immense resources of economic power which Britain discovered during the period naturally exalted her position and importance in international affairs. The mood of self-assertiveness which this exaltation induced was perfectly expressed by Palmerston. Disraeli (1804–81), in his handling of the 'Eastern Question' and of imperial affairs, continued Palmerstonian traditions in foreign policy. The years 1850–78 were years of great wars in Europe, but in only one of these – the costly and inconclusive Crimean War – was Britain directly concerned. Apart from various remote colonial and far eastern skirmishes, she contrived to retain her power without getting engaged in any of the other European Wars. With this exception the chief problems of her foreign policy were therefore the adjustments made necessary by such events as the revolutions of 1848, the American Civil War (1861–65), the three wars waged by Bismarck in his campaign to unite Germany by 'blood and iron', and the hostilities involved in the corresponding unification of Italy. The nature of Britain's international prestige can best be discovered by examining her attitude towards these turbulent events.

Perhaps the chief characteristic of Palmerston's attitude was a sturdy independence of judgement which took little account of sentiment or formality in diplomacy. Believing that it was for other Powers to seek and preserve British friendship and sympathy if they valued it, and that Britain herself need not court the favour of any Power in particular, he pursued what seemed at times an impulsive, temperamental, and inconsistent policy in Europe. He kept on good terms with Louis Philippe of France until he felt, in 1846, that Louis was taking an unreasonable line about French claims to the Spanish throne. He made his resentment plain, and within two years Louis was an exile in England. Though he had little liking or understanding of the liberal revolutionary and nationalist movements in Italy, Germany, and the Balkans, he was prepared to give them encouragement in the form of moral support. Though he valued the power of Austria as a counter-weight to Russian expansion westwards, he was willing to support Italian and Turkish defiance of Austria. His real concern was with preserving a certain balance of power in Europe as a whole, and if he showed sympathy for the Italian and German movements for national unification it was partly because he had little faith in the chances of their succeeding in their aims. Where he felt British prestige was involved he was just as ready to hurl thunderbolts against a small Power as against a great. The most famous example of this tendency was the somewhat ridiculous Don Pacifico incident of 1850.

Don Pacifico was a Portuguese money-lender who claimed that because he had been born in Gibraltar he was a British subject. When his house in Athens was pillaged he sought compensation from the Greek government, and when this was refused he sought Palmerston's aid. Without consulting France and Russia, who were joint guarantors with Britain of the independence of Greece, Palmerston sent British ships to blockade the Greek coast. The French ambassador was withdrawn from London, and when

Palmerston had to defend himself in Parliament against severe criticism of his methods he delivered himself of his famous 'Civis Romanus sum' speech. He claimed that 'a British subject, in whatever land he may be, shall feel confident that the watchful eye and the strong arm of England will protect him against injustice and wrong.' There is little doubt that Palmerston sincerely believed that a 'pax Britannica' had now replaced the old 'pax Romana'. In December, 1851, when Louis Napoleon, President of the Second French Republic, carried out a *coup d'état*, Palmerston without Cabinet knowledge or approval assured the French ambassador of his 'entire approbation' of the act. Even Lord John Russell's patience snapped, and he dismissed Palmerston from the post of Foreign Secretary. When two months later Lord Malmesbury became Foreign Secretary Palmerston told him he would soon discover 'what a power of prestige Britain possesses abroad', and that it would be his 'first duty to see that it does not wane.' That was, indeed, the chief preoccupation of his own policy.

During the fifties and sixties the three great forces at work in the world were liberalism, nationalism, and socialism. The first two struck sympathetic chords in Palmerston, as they did in the hearts of the prosperous British middle class. The third, as already described, left British politics almost unaffected until the seventies and eighties, despite the European activities of the First International and the part played by socialists in 1848 and by communists in 1871. Liberalism abroad to Palmerston and his middle-class supporters meant 'constitutionalism'. In 1841, *à propos* the establishment of a new Constitution in Greece, he wrote to Guizot: 'Her Majesty's Government do not happen to recollect any country in which a Constitutional system of Government has been established that has not on the whole been better off in consequence of that system than it had

been before.' In 1848 he saw the timely grant of constitu-
tional reforms by the ruler of Sardinia as a model for other
Italian monarchs. His support for nationalist movements
sprang partly from this affection for constitutionalism,
partly from a subtle regard for preserving the balance of
power in Europe. Two examples illustrate this. Regarding
Austrian rule in northern Italy as doomed in the face of
Italian national feeling, he wanted Charles Albert of
Sardinia to rule northern Italy constitutionally. He feared
French intervention in Italy against Austria. Although
Charles Albert failed in 1848–9, Palmerston steered
Britain safely through the tortuous diplomatic tangle which
ensued, and lived to see the Sardinian constitution become
the nucleus for united Italy. The Hungarian revolution of
1848 raised acutely a similar blend of liberal and international issues. He distinguished sharply between Austrian
power in Italy, which he regarded as untenable, and
Austrian power in Hungary, which he regarded as essential
to preservation of the balance of power, and therefore of all
political liberties, in Europe. 'The political independence
and liberties of Europe,' he declared in the House of
Commons in July, 1849, 'are bound up, in my opinion, with
the maintenance and integrity of Austria as a great European
Power.' Accordingly when the Hungarian revolution of
1848 was quelled only when Austria called in Russian help,
Palmerston found himself in a dilemma. Russian expansion
westwards was his greatest fear, and Austria was the main
bulwark. But British opinion sympathized strongly with the
defeated Hungarian rebels, and Palmerston had to conciliate this opinion whilst condoning Austria's brutal
oppression of Hungary and restraining Russian intervention. He found the answer in urging Austria to grant generous terms to Hungary – a general amnesty and restoration of
her constitution. Although his advice was little heeded, in

the sequel he was able to offer some protection to the exiled rebels. Kossuth and other revolutionaries fled from Hungary to Turkey, and so did exiles from Russian oppression in Poland. Austria and Russia again combined to demand that Turkey surrender these rebels. Britain and France sent ships to the Dardanelles and urged Turkey to refuse. Austria and Russia withdrew their demands. Again Palmerston was able to combine support for nationalist rebels, which was popular in Britain, with preservation of the balance of power, for Turkey was his other counter-weight to Russian expansion towards the Mediterranean. He was remarkably skilful in making the best of both worlds.

It was fear of Russian expansion, especially in the direction of the Mediterranean, and anxiety to uphold the declining Turkish Empire as a barrier to this expansion, which led Britain to take part in the Crimean War. To nationalists and constitutionalists alike it seemed intolerable that this despotic, aggressive Power, Russia, should pose as a sort of guardian of the Turkish Empire, with vague and convenient rights of interference. Turkish power extended over the whole Balkan peninsula, except Greece, as well as over Palestine. In the Balkans Russia claimed protection over the Christian and Slav subject peoples, and in Palestine both France and Russia claimed protection over the Holy Places, especially in Jerusalem itself. The British Ambassador in Turkey, Lord Stratford de Redcliffe, encouraged Turkey to make concessions over the Holy Places but to stand firm over the Balkans. Russia was furious, withdrew her ambassador, and war followed with Turkey in October, 1853. At the end of the month joint French and British fleets arrived again at the Dardanelles, and in March the following year they declared war on Russia. Within a year Sardinia joined them, seeking status as one of the Powers. The war lasted until 1856, cost Britain some 25,000 lives and

£70,000,000, and gave her no clear advantages beyond postponement of the break-up of Turkey. Palmerston, who did not resume power until early in 1855, had played a large part in leading that vocal part of British opinion which demanded war to teach the 'imperial bully' a lesson.

The Crimean War is an important landmark in the history of modern warfare. It was the last time that a British ambassador, unimpeded by telegraphic orders from home, could conduct a foreign policy of his own. It was the last big war to be fought without the resources of modern science. It brought, through the selfless labours of Florence Nightingale, a revolution in methods of nursing and medical supplies and equipment. It was the first time in Victorian England that the new force of middle-class politics, expressed through the press and public meeting, changed the foreign policy of the government. The Manchester School of liberals opposed the war. Cobden and Bright regarded it as unnecessary and unjustifiable. But middle-class opinion still followed Palmerston rather than Cobden in foreign affairs.

Similar internal divisions of public opinion appeared in Britain over the American Civil War which broke out in 1861. The ruling classes, especially the millowners and cotton merchants, regarded the secession of the southern States as another movement of national self-determination, and cherished strong sympathies for the southern aristocratic communities. They were comforted in the belief that slavery had nothing to do with the issue by the repeated declarations to this effect by Seward and Lincoln. The working classes in general, led by the Radicals, saw that slavery was an issue involved in the Civil War, and that the future of constitutional government and national unity lay with the forces of Lincoln and the North. Britain's basic diplomatic problem, once war had broken out, was whether she should recognize the Southern Confederacy. Lord John Russell and Gladstone were for recognition, and sympathized with the South. Palmerston wanted to take no step until the fighting proved more conclusive. Fortunately for the future of Anglo-American relations recognition was withheld until the issue became clearer, and was then never granted. The worst damage done was the widespread feeling in the North that Britain showed officially so little understanding for America in her hour of crisis. Friction developed over two maritime disputes concerning the *Trent* and the *Alabama*. A Northern naval officer forcibly took two Southern envoys, Mason and Slidell, from the *Trent*, which was a British ship. British indignation rose high: but, thanks to the intervention of Prince Albert, Russell's despatch was toned down and thanks to Abraham Lincoln's wisdom the dispute was overcome without war. The *Alabama* was a cruiser built in British yards and supplied to the South. She was very successful in attacking the commerce of the North before she was taken in June, 1864. The dispute about the supply of such ships to the South was settled only in 1872, by arbitration and payment of damages by Britain. It is remarkable that responsible ministers, backed by much ruling-class opinion, considered war between Britain and the North highly probable on several occasions during the Civil War.

During the years 1862–70 Prussia under Bismarck waged three successive wars as incidents in the unification of Germany. In 1863–4 Prussia and Austria jointly conquered the two little Duchies of Schleswig and Holstein which had long been attached to the Danish kingdom. Prussia took Schleswig, Austria Holstein. In July, 1863, Palmerston had said in the House of Commons, 'We are convinced – I am convinced at least – that if any violent attempt were made to overthrow these rights and interfere with that independence (i.e. of Denmark), those who made the attempt would find in the result, that it would not be Denmark alone with which they would have to contend.' But in the result both England and France had to stand aside. Bismarck now used the complex situation in the Duchies to pick a quarrel with his chief rival for German leadership, Austria. In a three-weeks' war, culminating in the victory of Sadowa in 1866, he defeated Austria. The northern States of Germany, led by Prussia, were formed into the North German Confederation, the southern States were grouped into an association 'with an independent international existence', and Austria was excluded from any further share in the organization of Germany. Four years later, in the Franco-German War, Bismarck succeeded in absorbing the southern States as well and in establishing the German Empire under Prussian leadership, with the Prussian King as its Emperor and himself as Imperial Chancellor. Palmerston had meanwhile died in 1865. His successors in office, Lord Clarendon and Lord Stanley, were forced to adopt a policy of 'non-intervention' in these dramatic events. Stanley declared, 'I am not a supporter of the system of advising foreign governments. I think this right has not only been used but abused of late, and that we have lost not gained by it.' Even the cherished Palmerstonian doctrine of preserving the integrity of the Turkish Empire was discarded. Stanley said that if the Turks 'disappeared from Europe he would not be inconsolable.' The complete revolution in the balance of power in Europe which was brought about by the appearance of a united German Empire coincided with a steep decline in British self-assertion in foreign affairs: and only after 1874 did Disraeli revive the older Palmerstonian tradition.

Britain showed similar complacency towards the unification of Italy. For both Germany and Italy the cultured and

intellectual classes had strong sympathies and even affections. The Court was by tradition and nature pro-German;
aristocratic and middle-class sympathies for the picturesque
and gallant fighters for Italian liberation and independence
were equally great. Lord John Russell and Palmerston both
favoured a unified kingdom in northern Italy, compounded
of Piedmont, Florence, and Modena, considering it 'an
excellent thing for that mechanical contrivance, the balance
of power.' Both, however, feared at first that a larger union
including Naples and Sicily, uniting southern and northern
Italy, would endanger the balance of power. They were won
round to acquiescing in this larger union only by the exploits
of Garibaldi and his Thousand. A last-moment decision of
Russell in favour of non-intervention restrained France
from intervening and left Garibaldi free to conquer Naples,
which he then transferred to the King of Sardinia and
Piedmont in 1860. Palmerston further declared, 'I think it
is quite impossible for us with a powerful fleet in the Mediterranean to stand by and see Spain crush by force of arms
the nascent liberties of Italy.' Russell, in his famous dispatch
of October 1860 which was published to the world, clinched
Britain's positive support for Italian unification. He urged
the principle that 'the Italians themselves are the best judges
of their own interests', adding that 'Her Majesty's Government can see no sufficient ground for the severe censure with
which Austria, France, Prussia, and Russia have visited the
acts of the King of Sardinia.' The dispatch won Britain the
affection of millions of Italians, but it involved open defiance
of all the major Powers of Europe. She was accused of
applauding rebellion and encouraging deposition of a ruler
by his subjects. She appeared, as clearly as in the days of
Canning, the champion of liberal and constitutional movements in Europe against the older order of despotism and
legitimist monarchy. Venice was joined to the new Italian

kingdom as a by-product of Bismarck's defeat of Austria in 1866, and Rome as a similar by-product of his defeat of France in 1870.

By 1871 the political map of Europe had been transformed. Instead of two clusters of weak States of assorted sizes there now stood two unified States, the German Empire and the Italian Kingdom. In 1815 there had been some thirty different German and Italian States, and the population, economic resources, and administration of the whole area remained splintered until 1871. Now there were two new and vigorous kingdoms, each under a popular national government eager to harness its wealth, manpower, and unified administration in the cause of national independence and expansion. The centre of gravity of power in Europe shifted eastwards, away from Britain and France. This shift of equilibrium affected France more immediately and dramatically than Britain. There were only 36 million Frenchmen in the world, but Britain had grown to a nation of 26 million, with a steady tide of emigration overseas, and Germany to 41 million. It affected Britain too in the long run. In the new Germany, especially, she met a formidable naval and industrial rival. By 1914 the ration of industrial potential between the three countries was estimated to be: Germany 3, Britain 2, France 1.

At the same time the United States, after a period of reconstruction and recovery following her Civil War, emerged as a great industrial Power and, in time, as a competitor to Britain in the markets of the world. In the seventies her chief influence on English economic life was exerted through her exports of corn. Sir John Clapham has summarized a complicated process like this:

> Each decade had seen some international dislocation which favoured the British farmer – a Crimean War, an American Civil War, a Russo-Turkish War (1877) – and until the late seventies

these dislocations, helped by the quick growth of population and the relatively backward state of transport, allowed increasing dependence on foreign grain supplies to accompany a reasonably well-sustained level of prices and of the acreage under corn. (*Economic History of Modern Britain*, Vol. II, p. 280.)

Already by 1875 nearly half the wheat consumed in Britain was imported from abroad, and the bad harvests of the late seventies increased the proportion to nearly 70 per cent.[1] The price of British wheat dropped greatly, contributing to the depression of British agriculture in these years. Britain was beginning to pay the penalty of industrial leadership, which was dependence for her food supplies on overseas producers. Her industrial output was, moreover, expanding much less rapidly than before. It has been roughly estimated that if her rate of expansion of industrial output in the early part of the century was 3 per cent per annum, it fell to under 2 per cent per annum in the last quarter of the century, and to about 1 per cent per annum in the first quarter of the twentieth century.

In these ways the picture of Britain's position internationally in the late 1870s is, therefore, one of diminished prestige, loss of initiative in foreign diplomacy, and increasing economic dependence on foreign supplies of food, though all these changes were at first masked by the continuing aura of prestige which lasted over from the middle of the century, and the continued pre-eminence of Britain financially and commercially in the world. She remained an immense exporter of money, men, and goods.

The Forces of Expansion

Much of Britain's weight in the world was felt not through her export of manufactured goods, but through her export

1. The proportion was thus reversed between 1850 and 1880.

of men and capital. Between 1853 and 1880 Britain sent out some 2,466,000 emigrants, of whom an unknown but probably small proportion returned. This amazing output had begun earlier and continued later than these dates, but that generation produced the bulk of British emigration. In 1849, at the time of the great Gold Rush, 300,000 people had left ports in the United Kingdom. In 1852, some 65,000 British people went out to Australasia. Most of this emigration was individual and unorganized, but various philanthropic organizations and trade unions helped. The most important official body was the Colonial Land and Emigration Commissioners which operated between 1847 and 1872, and tried to implement the doctrines of the colonial radicals, Lord Durham and Gibbon Wakefield, who regarded settlement as the very basis of the colonial empire. The reasons for this large-scale emigration were complex – partly economic and social, partly political, partly the simple search for adventure and fortune. By 1870 or so assisted emigration dropped out of fashion, and after that, though it continued in some strength, emigration was mainly a matter of individual enterprise and family connexion. Towards the end of the century the full tide of British expansionism in this respect too was at an ebb.

Export of capital was connected, though in intricate and often unpredictable ways, with export of men. By 1870 British capitalists had sunk some £800,000,000 abroad, whereas in 1850 the total had been only some £300,000,000. In 1872 alone £83,500,000 was invested abroad, and the total was more than quadrupled during the generation between 1850 and 1885. At least half these foreign investments were always in government securities, and borrowings were mostly by governments or for railways. London's chief rival was Paris but France's need to pay the huge indemnity demanded by Bismarck in 1871, and the way in which London weathered the financial crisis of 1873, kept Britain's financial lead over France. L. H. Jenks, in his study of *The Migration of British Capital to 1875*, has stated the real change which came over the international position of British financial investment by 1877: 'The export of a capital surplus was over. Her further investments were to come for a generation from the accruing profits of those which had already been made.' So in export of capital, too, the main tide of expansionism was ebbing by the late seventies.

As already mentioned, Britain's annual export of goods nearly trebled in value between 1850 and 1870, and so did her imports. As she grew in commercial power her excess of imports over exports increased, and this apparent 'unfavourable balance of trade' greatly worried her economists. The 'invisible exports' of shipping services and capital investment, for which foreigners had to pay, more than bridged the gap, at least until 1873. But during the last quarter of the century industrial competition from German and French mines and factories, as well as from American, meant that Britain was losing that old easy supremacy which she had enjoyed in the middle half of the century.

With the drop in prices from 1873 onwards her export values fell off rapidly, export quantities could not be greatly increased, but imports remained high. This produced a real adverse balance of trade which had to be covered by the surplus of capital which had previously been available for foreign investment. For the twenty years ending in 1874 Britain had exported an annual average surplus of capital of about £15,000,000. She had done this in addition to reinvesting abroad almost all the earnings received on existing foreign investments. These by the seventies had been about £50,000,000 a year. In 1876 and 1877 she collected income from her foreign investments for home consumption. Thus not only was the period of exporting a capital surplus at an end: but Britain was living to an ever greater extent on income from foreign investments which had previously been simply re-invested abroad. No change marks more decisively than this the end of her great era of economic expansion. Since 1815 British investors had achieved the remarkable feat of exporting a net capital surplus totalling about 500 million pounds, mostly during the years 1850–73. This fostered, as Jenks puts it, 'the growth of a rentier governing class, whose interests lay outside the community in which they lived and exerted influence.' From 1875 onwards income and capital tended to be withdrawn from Europe and transferred to South America, the United States, and British Dominions, and finally to the tropics and the Far East.

This coincidence of changes in British powers of expansion with the great changes in the international balance of power makes the 1870s a real turning-point in her fortunes. It was the prelude to the twentieth century, when she had to confront a new world seething with new forces, all challenging her old position. Her adjustments to meet these challenges, culminating in the First World War of 1914, are the theme of the final section of this book. Meanwhile the basis for consolidation of her expansion, in the shape of the new unity of the British Commonwealth of Nations, calls for some mention: for it was laid just at the climax of this central era of expansion, and laid, it might be said, just in time.

The British Empire

Canadian development, for which hopeful foundations had been laid by the Durham Report of 1839, reached its next landmark in 1867. The British North America Act of that year again separated Upper and Lower Canada but combined both with Nova Scotia and New Brunswick into one great confederation, the Dominion of Canada. The federal authority had more power than its counterpart in the United States, and within the next twenty years the provinces were welded into a new nation by the completion of the Canadian Pacific Railway and by wise and constructive government. It enabled the economic life of Canada to become more integrated, and less dependent on the markets of the United States. Manitoba joined the confederation in 1870, British Columbia in 1871, Prince Edward Island in 1873. Saskatchewan and Alberta were added in 1905. Control by London over the new Dominion rapidly diminished in practice from 1867 onwards, and 'Dominion status' came to mean what it means to-day – complete self-govenment and independence combined with voluntary but constant cooperation between the Dominion and United Kingdom Governments on all matters of common concern, and with close ties of affection and political solidarity.

India underwent a phase of great unrest and rapid change in this period. The great Governorship of Lord Dalhousie began, in 1849, with the annexation of the Punjab, and saw the completion of the framework of British India. In 1853 Macaulay's proposals for recruiting the Indian Civil Service by free competitive examination were adopted, and led to great loss of powers of patronage on the part of British politicians. The Mutiny (1857–8) led to formal abolition of the rule of the old East India Company in 1858, and the overhaul of the Indian Army by John Lawrence, who was Viceroy from 1864 to 1869. In 1876 Disraeli secured for Queen Victoria the new title of Empress of India.

In Australia, which by 1840 had some 130,000 white settlers, the discovery of gold at Ballarat in 1851 attracted large-scale immigration. By 1861 there existed four independent and self-govening colonies, New South Wales,

South Australia, Victoria, and Queensland, with about a million inhabitants among them. New Zealand was granted responsible government on the Canadian model in 1854, and had a population of a quarter of a million by 1870.

Responsible government was granted to Cape Colony in 1872 and to Natal in 1893. The scramble for Africa, in which Britain was to play a leading part, did not take place until the last decades of the century, and trouble with the Dutch settlers was stored up until the Boer War. But meanwhile Britain had so firm a footing in Africa that she would eventually hold her own as a leading Power there, and create the Union of South Africa as a British Dominion.

In these ways the most permanent results of this era of prestige and expansion were the creation of all the elements of the future British Commonwealth of Nations, and evolution of those principles of federalism and free cooperation through responsible government which were to produce a new kind of world-wide organization in our own times. Even when the economic reasons for her supremacy in mid-Victorian times were disappearing and a new world was taking shape, a new political and territorial basis for future power was being laid. It was to prove in many respects a more solid and durable basis than the pugnacity of Palmerston or the commercialism of Cobden.

CHAPTER IX

THE GROWTH OF THE MODERN STATE

The Monarchy

QUEEN VICTORIA left the British monarchy in a vastly stronger position than she found it. In 1837 when she came to the throne it had sunk low in popular esteem because of the character of her predecessors, George IV and William IV. The cautious and ominous remark of *The Times* leader-writer on her coronation expressed the prevailing attitude to the monarchy. Describing the welcome given by the people of London to the ceremony he wrote:

> They thought of her not as an individual to be loved with head-long zeal or played upon by corrupt adulation – their zealous and more generous reception of Her Majesty was from a higher and far more valuable motive. It was because they regarded her as in herself *an institution*. They saw the monarchy in Queen Victoria, and pledged themselves that for their own sakes they would uphold it, with the help of their Sovereign, so – if not, they would preserve the monarchy, in spite of an ill-advised monarch.

Contrast with this stiff phraseology that of *The Times* leader-writer of 1901, commenting on the death of the Queen.

> There are few among us who can recall the attitude of the people towards the Monarchy in the thirties and forties, but all have material enough to show them how striking is the contrast presented by the state of public opinion at the present day. We must not forget that many causes combined to effect a fundamental ameliora-

tion of the social conditions, and that many minds contributed to the triumph of larger and nobler conceptions of government. But, if we have had orderly evolution where other nations have gone through devastating internal conflicts, if the Monarchy held its own while new buttresses were being built for its support, and if it now stands not only broad-based upon the people's will, but strong in the affections of kindred nations overseas, we owe these results, to a degree which is hardly possible to over-estimate, to the womanly sweetness, the gentle sagacity, the utter disinterestedness, and the unassailable rectitude of the Queen.

Her achievement, indeed, was to transform the meaning of monarchy partly by her own good fortune but partly, too, by the force of her character and personality. Its appeal was no longer institutional. And just as the Hanoverian monarchs had brought monarchy into decline because of their personal characters, so Victoria exalted it and in so doing transformed it by her own personality.

The background to *The Times'* caution in 1837 is that disgust with preceding monarchs which it expressed so forcefully on the death of George IV in 1830:

> There never was an individual less regretted by his fellow-creatures than this deceased King. What eye has wept for him? What heart has heaved one sob of unmercenary sorrow?

The Spectator was hardly more complimentary on the death of William IV seven years later:

> His late Majesty, though at times a jovial and, for a king, an honest man, was a weak, ignorant, commonplace sort of person . . . Notwithstanding his feebleness of purpose and littleness of mind, his ignorance and his prejudices, William IV was to the last a popular sovereign, but his very popularity was acquired at the price of something like public contempt.

It was clear enough, by 1837, that the personality of the monarch could matter a great deal; it was also clear that the monarchy was surviving in spite of the monarchs. During the reign of Victoria it can be said that it survived only because of the monarch.

It was commonly assumed throughout the earlier nineteenth century that the survival of the monarchy, and with it aristocratic privilege as expressed in the House of Lords, would prove incompatible with the march of democracy and the achievement of universal suffrage. For that reason radicals and more extreme democrats were normally little opposed to the monarchy, because they thought it would perish in due course: and for the same reason the upper classes, and especially the House of Lords itself, resisted the progress of democracy as being likely to lead to republicanism. They were strengthened in this belief by the experience of the American Revolution and by the spectacle of nineteenth-century France. In 1854 the Crown was so bitterly attacked in the press that Victoria threatened to abdicate. During the Queen's period of gloomy seclusion after the death of Prince Albert in 1861 a strong tide of anti-monarchism grew in the country, resting on the argument that monarchy cost a lot and was not giving its money's worth in return. In 1867, when Walter Bagehot in his study of *The English Constitution* suggested very shrewdly that the real case for the monarchy now lay in its symbolic and emotional significance rather than in its actual political functions in the State, he could remark that 'it is nice to trace how the actions of a retired widow and an unemployed youth (the Prince of Wales) become of such importance.' In 1870–1 an English republican movement reached its greatest strength, men like Professor Fawcett and Sir Charles Dilke led a parliamentary campaign to probe into the Civil List, and fifty Republican Clubs were set up in Birmingham, Norwich, Cardiff, Plymouth, Aberdeen, and other towns.

The new kind of monarchy came into existence quite suddenly from 1871 onwards, with a curiously dramatic change of public opinion. In the autumn the Queen was ill. In November the Prince of Wales contracted a long and dangerous illness from the bad drains at Sandringham. It was the tenth anniversary of the Prince Consort's death from similar causes. On 14 December, the exact anniversary of Albert's death, the Prince made a sudden recovery. A great wave of popular sympathy swept England and on Boxing Day the Queen, for the first time in her life, issued a personal letter of thanks to her people. In February, 1872, a service of public thanksgiving was held at St Paul's, which was followed two days later by an attempt to assassinate the Queen. This killed the republican movement in England. 'What a sell for Dilke,' wrote a leading Conservative to Disraeli, 'this illness has been.' In June Disraeli made his famous Crystal Palace speech, exalting the Crown as the focus of the new Imperialism. Four years later he made Victoria Empress of India, and consolidated this new role for her. From then onwards her personal prestige and popularity were assured, and the new technique of monarchy was developed.

The two chief landmarks in this further development were the Golden Jubilee of 1887 and the Diamond Jubilee of 1897. Both were gigantic advertisements for the new Empire of which Victoria had come to be the crowned symbol, bringing enormous satisfaction to the masses and classes who felt that two generations of material progress and commercial expansion were now suitably summarized in these romantic pageants. To the first came representatives of the new self-governing Dominions and colonial Governors, Indian Rajahs and Burmese mandarins, Zulu chieftains and African headmen, representing the vastness and variety of the Empire. To the second came not only these again, but representatives of foreign Powers, halting their quarrels and enmities to join in homage to the old lady who was not only the Great White Queen but also the grandmother of Europe. If there was a somewhat autumnal atmosphere about these celebrations of Victorian glory, which shrewder observers detected as having some counterpart in the waning of British hegemony in Europe, yet they also symbolized the culmination of a reign of remarkable progress and expansion.

King Edward VII, a polished and brilliant man of the world by the time he came to the throne at the age of fifty-nine, enjoyed pomp and display and took a positive delight in lavish shows of every kind. He was cut out for ceremonial State occasions, and seized his opportunity to put the monarchy more in the front of public attention than it had been even during the last decades of Victoria's reign. He was less able and less industrious than his mother, but had probably a better understanding of the forces upon which a democratic and constitutional monarchy of the modern kind must rest. What he lacked in political experience and grasp he made up in natural dignity and charm, and a sense of tact in handling people. He gained an exaggerated reputation for influence on foreign policy, though his remarkable personal popularity in France played some part in achieving the *entente cordiale* with France in 1904. His social graces and accomplishments, combined with his sportsmanship, brought a new source of strength to the monarchy. His personality chimed with the more emancipated tastes and mood of the opening years of the new century. England, like the Prince himself, had come to feel a little stifled and cramped during the stuffy propriety of the Victorian age, and like him she came more into the open in her frank enjoyment of the pleasures of life. His death in 1910 was genuinely lamented by the mass of the people.

George V, who unlike his father was only forty-five when he came to the throne, had travelled widely, especially within the Empire, and brought to the tasks of kingship an unpretentious and quietly conscientious character. This proved excellently suited to the seriousness of the war-years; and during the years after 1918 he raised the monarchy, through his example of happy family life and through his highly effective tours and broadcasts, to an even higher pitch of prestige. The combination of dignity and popularity, of respect and affection, which he achieved won him a personal esteem which produced extraordinary scenes of genuine popular emotion during his illness, on the occasion of his Jubilee, and at his death. During his reign the 'Royal Family', and not merely the solitary figure of the King, became the symbol of monarchy. In an unsettled age of acute tensions, internal and international, the Royal Family served as a token of continuity and stability both within the United Kingdom and within the Empire.

Just as the succession of unattractive Hanoverians had brought monarchy into jeopardy, so the succession of attractive monarchs from Queen Victoria onwards created a new type of royal authority, resting not on constitutional prerogatives or political activity, but on the psychological needs of nationalism and imperialism and on the love of the masses of what Bagehot called 'nice and pretty events.' This development was of very obvious importance in the development of the British Commonealth: it was also of some significance in domestic affairs, because in the years after 1870 the country entered upon a period of political flux, economic dislocation, social tensions, and international crises, when a national anchorage to just such an institution as the new monarchy had a special value in providing stability. It is the aim of this chapter, and those which follow it, to examine some of the main causes and manifestations of this instability which threatened the generation before 1914.

The Mechanism of the Modern State

Although the period between 1875 and 1914 saw few innovations in the apparatus of government, it brought enormous changes in the meaning and working of old institutions. As already described, the reforms of Gladstone's first ministry laid the main foundations for the new kind of State which was to develop by 1914. The generation after 1875 built steadily on these foundations. The monarchy, ostensibly the same institution as in 1815, completely changed its role and its political significance in the British system of government; the House of Lords, ostensibly reduced in power only in certain particulars by 1911, in fact sank into a role of much less activity and importance than before; the House of Commons, becoming more completely than ever the true focus of legislative power, changed fundamentally its electoral basis and became more openly the organ of public opinion. Two Gladstonian Reform Bills of 1884 and 1885 extended the vote to agricultural workers and redistributed seats in favour of the larger at the expense of the smaller towns. They also increased the size of the Commons from 652 to 670 members. It was left to the Act of 1918 to remove all final anomalies in the male franchise and extend the vote to the majority of women: but these changes were in many respects inherent in the electoral changes of 1884–5. With secrecy of ballot after 1872 the workers of both town and country were able to use their vote freely without fear of reprisals from employer or landlord. Public opinion came to be more of a reality in politics. The growth of popular education after 1870 gave it greater reality.

No less important in the formation and guidance of public opinion was the rise of the new cheap popular press. Abolition of taxes on newspapers, advertisements, and paper between 1855 and 1861 paved the way. By 1870 there was a flourishing provincial daily press and a London press consisting of penny dailies such as the *Daily Telegraph*, the *Standard* (both Conservative), and the *Daily News* (Liberal). The *Daily Chronicle* (Liberal) was added in 1877. *The Times* sold at threepence. Written for the upper and middle classes and owned as private family concerns, these London dailies were essentially political organs. The monthly and quarterly reviews, such as the *Fortnightly Review* and the *Saturday Review*, catered for a similarly well-informed and selective public. In 1880 George Newnes founded *Tit-Bits* to catch the new popularly educated classes, and in 1894 Kennedy Jones launched a new version of the *Evening News* as a halfpenny evening paper. The big revolution came two years later when Kennedy Jones and Alfred Harmsworth (later Lord Northcliffe) started the *Daily Mail* as a halfpenny morning paper aiming at a new scale of circulation. Instead of printing news reports as they came in, the *Mail* had them written up into spicy news-stories, all ready for easy consumption. Though Lord Salisbury scornfully described it as 'written by office-boys for office-boys' it was exactly tuned to the public taste of half-educated business men and women and of the newly-educated masses. It set a new standard in sensational journalism and therefore also in size of circulation and value of advertisements. It was the model for several later creations of our own times.

The two branches of government which most expanded in size and functions during these years were on the one hand the civil service and on the other local government authorities. The extension of governmental control and organization of economic and social life made both these developments inevitable, and it was of immense importance for our modern constitution that they developed simultaneously and in due proportion to one another. Expansion of the central administration out of proportion to the expansion of local government activities would have led to a much more highly centralized and bureaucratic State. If the growth of municipal enterprise and of 'gas-and-water social-ism' was mainly due to pressure from radicals and socialists such as Joseph Chamberlain at Birmingham and the Fabians in London, the growth of the civil service was entirely haphazard and due to necessities of practical administra-tion.

The Privy Council was, at first, the normal repository of every kind of new duty of supervision over public services. By 1880, as Mr K. B. Smellie has remarked, its functions could only be classified alphabetically.

> It was responsible for assizes, burial boards, charters of boroughs, clergy returns, coinage currency, contagious diseases of animals, convocation, county courts, Dentistry Acts, Education Acts, gas company amalgamations, etc., to the end of the alphabet. (*A Hundred Years of English Government*, p. 253.)

The Home Office, too, was used in this omnibus fashion. It was responsible for enforcement of the regulations of the early Factory Acts, control of industrial diseases, the manu-facture of explosives, safety in mines, the Workmen's Compensation Act of 1906, the Employment of Children Act, and so on, to responsibility for the protection of wild flowers and control of advertisements and money-lenders.

One important tendency of administrative development was for special Boards, on the model of the Board of Trade, to take over groups of such duties formerly performed by the Privy Council or the Home Office. In 1889 the Board of Agriculture took over the agricultural duties of the Council and of various Commissioners: in 1903 it became the Board of Agriculture and Fisheries. Ten years later the old Department of Education split away from the Council and became the Board of Education. The Local Government Board dated from 1870. By 1914 the civil service was recruiting boy clerks direct from the elementary schools and a new intermediate class of executive officers from the secondary schools. Administrative grades were filled, after 1870, by competitive examinations at University level. The rapid extension of social services by 1914 involved naturally great increase in the size of the service. Whereas some 21,300 had sufficed in 1832, more than 50,000 were employed by 1880 (excluding the staff of the telephone and telegraph services), and by 1914 some 280,000, including Scotland and Ireland as well as England and Wales, and including the staff of the General Post Office. Multiplication of the number of civil servants by five within the generation previous to 1914 is one index of the new functions being performed by the modern State.

A further equally important tendency, besides mere growth in size and complexity, was the grant by Parliament of much wider discretionary powers to Ministers and their departments. From 1870 onwards the habit grew of relieving the congestion of parliamentary business by providing that the details of Bills should be filled in departmentally. Now that legislation so often concerned matters involving scientific or technical knowledge this was inevitable. What has come to be known as 'delegated legislation', about which there has been prolonged controversy and a famous Parliamentary Committee's report, assumed large proportions only after the establishment of the Boards of Agriculture and Education. As this fact suggests, it is a natural outcrop of social legislation. So much had to be done, affecting the everday life of the ordinary citizen, that it was quite impossible for Parliament, engaged as it was in an increasing bulk of law-making, to lay down precise details of every new provision. This had to be left to the discretionary power of responsible Ministers, and to that of their ever-growing staffs. Naturally, again, the spate of new social legislation produced by the Liberal Governments of 1906–14, providing old age pensions, labour exchanges, and national health insurance, meant a new and unprecedented extension of delegated legislation. That process has continued ever since.

In step with these striking developments in central government, the machinery of local government was completely overhauled. Although municipal councils, elected by rate-payers, had been set up for the towns in 1835, the counties were still formally, in 1870, governed by the Justices of the Peace in petty and quarter sessions. The growth of social legislation from the new poor law onwards had led, however, to an amazing multiplicity of special local authorities, often with overlapping and confused duties and areas. By the eighties it was also plainly absurd that country-dwellers who were expected, through their parliamentary vote, to judge great issues of national, foreign, or imperial policy should still have no say in determining the government of their own locality. The obvious answer was to set up elected County Councils on the pattern of the Borough Councils, and this was done in 1888. To the new councils were transferred all the administrative duties hitherto carried out by the un-elected Justices of the Peace, and many of those being performed by the piecemeal sanitary and educational boards. To meet the objections of the large towns to having any of their local services provided by County Councils, a special category of County Boroughs was created, having all the powers of a County Council and therefore immune from County interference. Some sixty big towns gained this status. Outside them, the county system was subdivided into urban and rural districts. London, always a very special problem, was ranked as a County, and a London County Council was set up, its area being defined by carving out pieces from the three counties adjacent to the capital.

The larger boroughs headed by Birmingham, whose Mayor from 1873 to 1876 was the enterprising Joseph Chamberlain, and the London County Council, strongly influenced by Fabian Socialists like Sidney Webb, immediately showed how effectively and extensively local authorities could provide social services for their citizens. Muncipal socialism preceded national socialism, in practice, by nearly half a century. The Municipal Corporations Act of 1882 swept away the last legal restrictions on services which municipal bodies could undertake, and another Act, two years before, removed the property qualification for town councillors and made any householder eligible for election. The result was amusingly described by Sidney and Beatrice Webb:

> The individualist town councillor will walk along the municipal pavement, lit by municipal light and cleansed by municipal brooms with municipal water and – seeing by the municipal clock in the municipal market, that he is too early to meet his children coming from the municipal school, hard by the county lunatic asylum and the municipal hospital, will use the national telegraph system to tell them not to walk through the municipal park, but to come by the municipal tramway to meet him in the municipal reading-room, by the municipal museum, art-gallery, and library, where he intends ... to prepare his next speech in the municipal town hall in favour of the nationalization of canals and the increase of Government control over the railway system. 'Socialism, Sir,' he will say, 'don't waste the time of a practical man by your fantastic absurdities. Self-help, Sir, individual self-help, that's what has made our city what it is.'

Political Flux

The parliamentary scene from 1875 until the end of Victoria's reign was dominated more by the Irish Question than by any other. The chief reason for this was the conversion of Gladstone to Home Rule for Ireland, and the effects which this conversion had on the Liberal and Conservative parties. The repercussions of the Irish Question mingled with the forces of the new imperialism to transform the old party alignments even before the new Labour Party appeared on the scene in any strength. It is possible only briefly to indicate the main sorts of political change which resulted from these events.

The interlude of the Gladstone-Disraeli duel, which has been already discussed, came to an end personally in 1881 when Disraeli died, and politically in 1885 when Lord Salisbury's Conservative ministry inaugurated what proved to be a phase of predominantly Conservative government. Conservatives ruled continuously from 1885 until 1905, except for breaks of a few months in 1886, and of less than three years between 1892 and 1895. During his one great ministry of 1874–80 Disraeli laid a new basis of Conservative policy. The party could reckon on its old landed and Church interest for support, and to some extent on large elements in the middle classes which had been alienated from the Liberals by the Education Act of 1870 and by the disestablishment of the Irish Church. It also won support from conservative working men, to many of whom Disraeli had given the vote in 1867, and Disraeli set himself to strengthen this section of his Party's support. He concentrated on social reform which Gladstone had personally neglected, and passed acts dealing with artisans' dwelling-houses, public health, factory regulation, and trade unions. Public education was made compulsory but not yet free in 1880. But increasingly he became absorbed in foreign and imperial affairs. Trouble broke out again in the Balkans in 1875 and there was the scare of a European War. Russian intrigues in Afghanistan led to British intervention and war, and to a revival of the Palmerstonian dread of Russian expansion. By timely diplomatic intervention in the Russo-Turkish War Disraeli gained Cyprus for the British Crown and claimed to have brought back 'peace with honour'. By purchase of the Suez Canal shares and the proclamation of Victoria as Empress of India at the Delhi Durbar he led the Conservative Party back to a more positive interest in imperialism. The economic depression and the agricultural slump of the late seventies revived the old policy of protectionism within the Conservative ranks, under the slogan of 'fair trade'. Disraeli's ministry is important because it came at this moment of composite crisis in British fortunes, and because Disraeli used that moment to infuse Conservatism with a new and more active policy at home and overseas. He laid the basis for Conservative hegemony during the next fifteen years.

It was the Irish Question and Gladstone's conversion to Home Rule which completed the transformation of the political scene. Throughout the century Ireland had been the greatest single source of violence and political upheaval in English politics. Daniel O'Connell's Catholic Association for promoting Roman Catholic emancipation in the 1820s had been followed by the 'Young Ireland' movement of the 1840s and the crisis of the potato-famine in 1846; by Fenianism, drawing funds and strength from the American Irish, in the 1860s; by the Land League with its encouragement of agrarian outrages, and by the Home Rule League of Charles Stewart Parnell, in the 1870s. All Gladstone's efforts to remedy the situation by the Disestablishment of the Irish Church (1869), the Land Act (1881), and the Arrears Act (1882) left the raw sore of fierce Irish nationalism, now content with nothing short of Home Rule, and likely in the end to demand total independence and separation from Great Britain. Parnell's technique of obstruction and 'filibustering' in the English Parliament, where he used his highly disciplined group of Irish members to prove that England would not be allowed to govern her-

self until she let Ireland govern herself, brought the Irish
Question into the forefront of British parliamentary politics.
After 1882 Gladstone was converted to the belief that Ireland must be given Home Rule, and he came into office in
1886 pledged to Home Rule. This split the Liberal Party,
for the Whig section, led by Hartington, deserted Gladstone,
and the Radical section, led by Joseph Chamberlain, dis-
approved of the actual terms of Gladstone's first bill. When
the bill was consequently defeated Gladstone appealed to
the country in the general elections of 1886 and lost. A
Conservative and Liberal-Unionist government under Lord
Salisbury took office and it was clear, as Salisbury remarked,
that 'politics are Ireland'. Gladstone's second bill of 1893
was rejected by the House of Lords, and the failure of the
constitutional Home Rule movement gave rise, at the end
of the century, to the birth of Sinn Fein, a more extreme
Irish nationalist movement demanding an independent
Republic.

The Irish problem was to haunt British politics until 1914,
because it continued to cause a deep split both between and
within English political parties. A parliamentary Irish
Nationalist Party, led by John Redmond, went on: but outside it formed various extreme and violent movements like
Sinn Fein, the Irish Republican Brotherhood, the Gaelic
League, and the highly syndicalist Labour Movement. The
growth of distinct Protestant consciousness in Ulster and
the notion of partition should Home Rule be achieved threw
both the English parties into great disarray. The Conservative Unionist Party supported Ulster's independence
as a spoke in the wheel of Home Rule, while the Liberal
Party found itself led to coerce Ulster in the cause of Home
Rule. The Home Rule bill moved by the Liberals in 1912
proposed a separate Parliament for Ireland and con-
templated even separate Parliaments for England, Wales,

and Scotland, but wanted to keep one Imperial Parliament also at Westminster. It was federalist in idea, because federalism was popular after its success in the United States, Canada, and Australia. Party differences thus came to assume a fundamental character, involving totally different conceptions of the future of the British Commonwealth. Even more significantly, both parties found themselves urging courses of violence, and the whole tradition of constitutional parliamentary government in Britain was brought into jeopardy. Bonar Law exhorted the army in Dublin to mutiny rather than coerce Ulster, Asquith failed to prevent the import of arms to the Ulster and Dublin volunteers, and Lord Willoughby de Broke, a diehard Unionist, urged the House of Lords, on the brink of 1914, to refuse to pass the Army Annual Act. The twentieth century, an era of violence, opened with a decade of violence and a sudden decadence in parliamentary habits.

The violence of the conflict between parties broke out also over the problem of the powers of the House of Lords. The Conservative Party had a deeply entrenched majority in the Lords, and throughout the century the Lords had repeatedly resisted political and social reforms. The first Reform Bill had been passed only under threat that the King would create enough new peers to swamp the Tory majority. Gladstone's efforts to secure Home Rule for Ireland had been frustrated by the Lords. Conflict between the two Houses of Parliament reached a crisis in 1906 when a large Liberal majority was returned in the general elections and the new Labour Party first appeared in strength. A bill to abolish plural voting was passed by large majorities of three-to-one and four-to-one in the Commons but was rejected by the Lords. It became clear that Liberal government was impossible, however strong its electoral support, so long as the Unionists retained so complete a grip on the

Lords. Schemes began to be put forward for reform of the upper House and for restriction of its powers. Throughout the parliament of 1906–10 Liberal measures were constantly amended or blocked in the Lords, and every bill which was opposed in the Commons on its third reading was then rejected by the Lords. In November, 1909, they precipitated the crisis by rejecting Lloyd George's budget until it should be submitted to the judgement of the electorate. This meant either a claim to amend money bills, which had been for long resisted by the Commons, or else a claim to force on the King and Commons a dissolution of Parliament although the existing government had a huge majority in the Commons. In the consequent two sets of general elections in January and December, 1910, Liberals and Unionists found themselves almost equal in parliamentary strength, but the support of the forty and more Labour Party representatives and of most of the Irish Nationalist group of eighty gave the Liberals a very decisive majority. Edward VII died in May, but efforts to find a compromise which would avoid confronting the new King with a constitutional deadlock came to nothing. Only the threat that George V would be willing to create enough new peers to swamp the Lords ensured that the Government's Parliament Bill passed the Lords: and since more than 400 new peers would have had to be created, the situation had become somewhat ridiculous. Even so there was a diehard wing of the Unionist Party, led by Lord Willoughby de Broke and Austen Chamberlain, which wanted to force the Liberals to carry out the threat rather than surrender the power of the Lords.

As with Ireland, the particular formal issue between parties concealed an underlying difference of general constitutional principle. Was the British Parliament to be a really bi-cameral institution, as the Unionists wanted? If so, they agreed that the composition of the upper House would have to be changed, and wanted this reform as an alternative to a diminution of the Lord's powers. Or was it to be fundamentally a uni-cameral institution, with the powers of the upper House so attenuated that the will of the Commons would always in the end prevail? This the Liberals wanted, and if they were to have their way the Parliament Bill must go through, defining more narrowly the exact legislative powers of the Lords. The Parliament Act eventually became law in 1911. It removed control over Money Bills from the Lords, and left it to the Speaker of the House of Commons to decide which bills should count as Money Bills. It restricted control of the Lords over other legislation to a maximum delaying power of two years. In return it shortened the maximum life of a Parliament to five years instead of seven. Its preamble left both parties committed to a further reform of the composition of the upper House, which has never since been carried out. The Conservative Party, acting through the House of Lords, had conducted what Professor E. L. Woodward has called 'a sedate sort of strike against the Constitution.' But there were moments when it was far from sedate: and the whole controversy was conducted on both sides with such extreme heat and violence that it was clear, in this respect too, that British politics had entered a new and more violent phase with the coming of the twentieth century.

The other main feature of parliamentary development in these years was the arrival on the political stage of the Labour Party. Its solid basis was the growing trade union movement, although the Trades Union Congress was joined, in its creation of the Labour Representation Committee, by the Fabian Society (founded in 1884), the Independent Labour Party (founded in 1893 by Keir Hardie), and the Social Democratic Federation (founded in 1881 by H. M.

Hyndman). The Labour Representation Committee, dating from 1900, put up fity-one candidates in the general elections of 1906 and twenty-nine of them got in. After this victory it changed its name to the Labour Party, and from that time onwards there has always been a Labour Party in Parliament. By 1900 trade-union membership in Britain topped the two million mark, and it included a mass of unskilled as well as of skilled labour. The late eighties and the nineties were a period of great strikes in industry, ranging from the famous London Dock strike of 1889 to the Engineers' strike of 1897. Though the new Labour Party did much to guide the energies of this mighty new movement into constitutional and parliamentary channels, an immediate result of trade union growth was a phase of industrial unrest and violence. Here again, as in France of the same years, elements of violence played an increasing part in social life.

A similar tendency was reflected in the growing feminist movement. The demand for extension of the vote to women was nineteenth-century in origin. John Stuart Mill had come to favour it. In 1903 the Women's Social and Political Union was founded at Manchester by Mrs Pankhurst with strong affiliations with the Independent Labour Party; and in 1908 a secessionist group from this movement formed the Women's Freedom League. Both movements were militant, seeking to draw attention to their grievances by interrupting political meetings, breaking windows, and chaining their members to railings. Imprisonment led to hunger-strikes, and hunger-strikes to forcible feeding. From 1912 onwards the extremists, led by Christabel Pankhurst from Paris, resorted to organizing a veritable wave of crime which included such offences as arson, false fire-alarms, cutting telephone-wires, slashing pictures in public galleries, and throwing bombs. From 1913 onwards this degree of violence came to be discredited, and the more constructive and law-abiding body, the National Union of Women's Suffrage Societies, was formed. In 1918 the Representation of the People Act gave the vote to all women over thirty years of age, who then numbered some 8,500,000.

It is the features which all these political developments have in common which are most significant. Most obviously, there is the resort to open violence. It is no accident that within ten years so conservative and sedate a body as the House of Lords could witness scenes of hysterical resistance to a moderate diminution of its powers; so traditionally 'constitutional' party as the Conservatives could openly support mutiny in the Army; so traditionally passive a section of the population as the Edwardian women could find themselves fighting police and burning houses; and so traditionally democratic a body as organized labour could find itself engaged in recurrent strikes and even sabotage. There is a universal note of desperation, of hysteria, of pent-up passion, in all these events of the decade before 1914. If Ireland had become a synonym for unrest, it was new that two armed parties should be on the brink of civil war when they were interrupted by the outbreak of a world war. Mr George Dangerfield, in his spirited and valuable study of *The Strange Death of Liberal England*, has examined the connexion between all these 'rebellions' which reached simultaneous crescendo in the years 1910–14.

> For the assaults upon Parliament of the Tories, the women, and the workers have something profoundly in common. In each case, a certain conscious security was in question . . . The workers did not want to be safe any more; they wanted to live, to take chances, to throw caution to the winds: they had been repressed too long. And so the deepest impulse in the great strike movement of 1910–14 was an unconscious one, an enormous energy pressing up from the depths of the soul; and Parliament shuddered before it, and under its impact Liberal England died.

It might be added that similar psychological impulses can be detected in the irrationalism of the Boer War a decade earlier, in the sensationalism of the journalism and literature of the time, and in the panics and war-scares of the whole generation. If the period brought a more insistent demand for fresh forms of 'social security' it also, paradoxically, saw a deep and bitter revolt against the older forms of security. There was a dynamic new energy at work, transforming the face and character of England, and impatiently brushing aside in the process the more stately and leisurely modes of constitutional government, and with them the habits and ideology of Victorian Liberalism. 'Freedom' and 'emancipation' were still the slogans: freedom for Ireland, freedom for Ulster; freedom for women and freedom for the workers; but the important problems of how these diverse freedoms were to be reconciled with one another, and how all of them were to be reconciled with the freedoms achieved by parliamentary constitutional government, were not considered at all. Because these questions were left unanswered parliamentary government fell into decline. Again paradoxically, it was saved only by the outbreak of the greatest convulsion of all, which rallied militant Ireland, militant suffragettes, and militant workers alike, in defence of the nation. Some of the hidden springs of these strange movements, however, can be discovered by looking further at the changes in the social environment amid which they took place, and at the other manifestations of the new spirit in imperial and foreign affairs.

CHAPTER X

THE DEMAND FOR SOCIAL SECURITY

A Town-bred Population

IT was during the generation after Waterloo that the balance of English economic and social life changed from being predominantly agricultural to being predominantly industrial; and with this change, as was shown in the earlier section of this book, came the growth of urbanization, the development of the mine and factory as the unit of production, and the transformation of the 'average' Englishman into a townsman rather than a countryman. This change took the whole of the nineteenth century to work itself out. By the end of it Britain had clearly become an industrial State, depending for its living on manufacturing raw materials – many of which came from abroad – and on exporting a large proportion of the finished products. This meant that the economic life of England was now intricately and closely linked with international trade and with world economic changes. The fact was first brought vividly home to Englishmen in the mid-seventies, when the price-fall and the depression in agriculture produced social effects in England which few had foreseen, none could prevent, and all found perplexing. The combination of simultaneous changes described above (Chapter VIII) meant that the Englishman was now nakedly at the mercy of vast economic changes beyond the control of his own government. He had the vote, and could at elections choose between alternative governments: but if none of these governments could provide for him the social security he desired, what was the vote worth? The bloom on the grapes of Liberalism was fading at the moment of their coming to maturity. More and more the working classes began to turn to forms of organization other than the State, and to political beliefs other than Liberalism and Radicalism, in the search for more effective protection of their rights and welfare.

On one hand, there were the trade unions; and the closing decades of the century and the years before 1914 were a period of large-scale industrial unrest. In France syndicalism was already challenging the authority of the State. In 1906 Georges Sorel provided Frenchmen with a ready-made creed of revolutionary syndicalism in his work bearing the ominous title *Reflections on Violence*. Sorel and his followers found no disciples of importance in England. But organized trade unionism confronted governments in England with very much the same problems as did the syndicalist labour movements in France. In England Fabians and Guild Socialists evolved theories which seemed to adapt democratic doctrines to the realities of modern industrial conditions, and wrote of workers' participation in the management of industry and of 'industrial democracy'.[1] There was still, of course, a wide gulf between these theorists and the rank-and-file trade unionists whose chief concern was that collective bargaining with employers for better working-conditions or higher wages should be successful. There was also a gulf between the already very sober trade union leaders and the Trades Union Congress on one hand, and the sponsors of countless 'unofficial strikes' on the other. The industrial unrest was throwing up its own leaders, and only a few of the political socialist leaders, such as Tom Mann, George Lansbury, and Ben Tillett, were actively connected

1. e.g. *Industrial Democracy* by Sidney and Beatrice Webb; *Self-Government in Industry* by G. D. H. Cole.

with it. Hopes of progress were now increasingly pinned on either direct action with the weapons of strike and boycott, or collective bargaining through organizations to which the State was only then giving full legal recognition and protection. But the sharp check in the rise of real wages between 1900 and 1913 was due to economic crisis which such weapons had little power to remedy.

On the other hand, there was the parliamentary Labour Party. Its immediate potentialities as a force for achieving social reforms were at first exaggerated: it was not realized how much even the small Labour Party in Parliament depended on Liberal votes for its existence and on Liberal Party support for fulfilment of any portion of its programme. But its long-range potentialities were clear enough. Other working-class movements were also gaining strength. The Cooperative movement flourished. In 1903 the Workers' Educational Association was founded, and by 1914 it had 179 branches and 11,430 individual members. Ruskin Hall was started at Oxford in 1899. The creation of a separate political party, drawing most of its strength from labour organizations and existing to promote especially the interests and welfare of the working classes, was a momentous new factor in British politics. It directed trade union energies and hopes into constitutional and parliamentary channels, and offered some definite promise that in time the social welfare and security of the masses would be made matters of specific and systematic legislation. It is no accident that, after decades of unsuccessful experiments, it was during these years of economic crisis that a Labour Party of some significance entered the stage.

The most important consequences in the short run were that both the older political parties began to compete more feverishly for working-class votes by efforts to provide greater social and economic security through legislation.

The Liberal Party, influenced more and more by Lloyd George, launched its programme of social reform most of which it achieved, with the help of the Labour Party, between 1906 and 1914. The forces of social liberalism and of liberal socialism came together, and achieved a remarkable series of new measures within eight years. The Conservatives, re-infused with reforming zeal by the conversion of Joseph Chamberlain to the doctrines of tariff reform, urged a policy of systematic protection for British industries in a world where one market after another was being closed to British exports. Free trade was dying, because the temporary conditions which had made it possible and profitable were passing away. The ultimate reasons for these new policies lay in world economic conditions: but the immediate reasons why all British political parties adopted them at this time lay in the outlook of the new generation of town-bred Englishmen, conscious in a way that their fathers were not of the problems both human and economic which confronted an urban civilization. The normal community in England was now no longer a village, but an industrial town. The horizon of Englishmen in their daily life and work was not the open fields but the sky-line of roof-tops and chimney-stacks. The home was not for most a country house or a cottage, but a town villa or tenement. Conditioned by these changes to be more gregarious, to seek their pleasures more collectively and their security through large-scale organization, the new human content of England demanded rapid adjustments in its political and social framework. But for the outbreak of war in 1914 these adjustments might have come more smoothly: it is doubtful if they would have come more quickly. For the war, by heightening national consciousness and by demonstrating what modern methods of organization could achieve, in the end strengthened existing tendencies. The English proletariat was rapidly taking shape, though its aims and its spirit were not exactly those which Karl Marx had expected or hoped.

Economic Crisis

In Germany Bismarck had shown that one way to revive Conservatism was to adopt a policy of social reform, and that one way to pay for social services was through a policy of fiscal protection. Other European countries tended to follow his example, and European markets became closed to British goods. Meanwhile European industries were being built up, behind this protection, to rival British producers in world markets. In 1890 the United States adopted the MacKinley tariff, a rigorous system of protection. Two years later the English Conservative leader, Lord Salisbury, suggested that tariffs as a method of reprisals, if only to get other countries to reduce their tariffs, might be justified. The Conservative slogan was now 'fair trade', not 'free trade', however much 'free trade' might still be hailed as the ideal. At the turn of the century trade recovered for a time. In 1900 the total value of British exports rose to £291,192,000, as compared with the previous maximum of £256,257,000 in 1872, before the slump. Although the figure dropped in succeeding years it remained at a high level until 1905. But this increase was mainly due to one industry – coal – and its huge increase masked the stagnation in the textile industries and the positive decline in the iron and steel industries, where German and American home industries were replacing imports from Britain. Meanwhile the crisis in agriculture intensified and prices went on falling. It was mainly due to the immense increase of cultivation in the United States, Canada, and Argentina, combined with the development of railways and steamships and the lowering of freight charges. The movement of labour to the towns was depopulating the countryside; the number of agricultural labourers and farm servants dropped from 983,919 in 1881 to only 689,292 in 1901. Better-paid posts in the towns, as policemen, railwaymen, or municipal employees, were attracting the less well-paid labourers away from the farms. The spread of elementary education made them more discontented with their lot. In part as a consequence of this, the area of land under cultivation in the United Kingdom fell from nearly $8\frac{1}{4}$ million acres in 1871 to just over $5\frac{3}{4}$ million acres in 1901: though the acreage of pasture rose between the same dates from over $11\frac{1}{4}$ million to more than $15\frac{1}{4}$ million acres. Pasture farming was beginning to suffer from the competition of the frozen meat imported from Australia and New Zealand, and dairy-farming from the butter imported from Canada, Denmark, and Holland. Even the character of the landed gentry was changing. Their income came from stocks and shares. Often they did not live in the country to make money, but only visited it to spend money. The new forms of local government were often resented by the farmers, who grumbled that the money they paid in rates was spent on the local towns, and that the expensive new elementary schools robbed them of labour.

Meanwhile much of the labour drawn away from the countryside was unemployed. Unemployment figures were high in the eighties; they fell between 1894 and 1899, during the revival of trade, but rose again between 1900 and 1904. In the nineties Charles Booth investigated pauperism in London and several parliamentary committees studied remedies for unemployment. In 1902 the London boroughs were empowered to set up labour bureaux. The old questions of 'poor relief' arose again in a more acute form, and now public opinion demanded more systematic handling of them. The Unemployed Workmen Act of 1905 gave the

Local Government Board power to establish committees like those of London in other towns. These committees were to keep a register of the unemployed and to establish labour exchanges. They might not spend money in wages or maintenance unless funds were freely contributed by the public, but an appeal for funds realized £125,000 by the end of the year. So a definite, if cautious and inadequate, beginning had been made in the development of governmental responsibility for unemployed people. Analysing the registers so compiled, William Beveridge, in his book *Unemployment* (1909), showed that unemployment was usually due to casual employment. In that year the Liberals passed an Act establishing labour exchanges all over the country, and two years later a separate section of the National Insurance Act provided for contributory insurance against unemployment. The machinery of the Ministry of Labour was created before 1914, although the Ministry itself was not set up until two years later.

One index of the slowing down of economic development at the end of the nineteenth century is the quite sudden check in the growth of the country's aggregate income. After 1880 it increased more rapidly than the population, and in 1900 it was about one-third greater than it had been twenty years earlier. But it stayed at practically the figure of 1900 for the next fourteen years, which helps to explain the period of labour unrest just before 1914. The power of trade unions, the establishment of national health insurance and of other social services (including municipal as well as national), and the increase in income tax and death duties, all helped to distribute wealth more evenly. These took time to produce the effect, and the immediate result was discontent.

The Origins of Social Security

The first manifestation of this discontent was anxiety for the protection and extension of trade-union rights. Unless full freedom of association were secured workers' organizations would not be able to play their full part in improving conditions and in providing some measure of social security for their members. The position by the end of Gladstone's first ministry has already been described (above, p. 148). The most serious challenges of the growth of trade unions now came from two legal decisions. In 1901, in the case of the Taff Vale Railway Company *v.* the Amalgamated Society of Railway Servants, the House of Lords decided against what had been the common assumption since the legislation of 1871, that a trade union could not be sued for damages arising out of industrial disputes. Were corporate trade union funds to be made legally liable to stand damages caused by a strike, the unions' chief sanction in collective bargaining would be virtually destroyed. In the Taff Vale case the union concerned had to pay £23,000 in damages and the legal expenses came to even more. Other legal disputes at this time still further narrowed union powers. The unions began an intensive campaign to get the decision reversed by Act of Parliament, and they eventually succeeded in 1906. The Trade Disputes Act gave complete protection against judgements like the Taff Vale decision. It also confirmed the right of 'peaceful picketing' allowed since 1875. Three years later another decision of the Lords, known as the 'Osborne judgement', denied that trade unions had the right to spend any part of their funsd on political objects. This decision struck at the very basis of the new Labour Party. The Trade Union Act of 1913 restored political rights to the unions. Any union could now take political action provided that it first obtained the authority of its members by a ballot vote, and provided that it allowed any members who wished to 'contract out' from the levy for the political fund.

The second and more spectacular manifestation of discontent was the large number of strikes, reaching unprecedented number and scale, which occurred both with and without trade-union backing. There was a lull after the big strikes of the 1890s, until the crescendo of 1910–12. This climax was produced partly by the infiltration of syndicalist ideas from France, encouraged by the two decisions of the Lords already mentioned: these seemed to bear out the syndicalist argument that strikes and sabotage were the only weapons likely to coerce the ruling classes into recognizing trade-union rights. In 1910 a sympathetic strike broke out in South Wales, affecting 30,000 mineworkers. Police and troops had to quell the consequent riots. In 1911 there was an epidemic of strikes among shipworkers and dockers for higher wages, and they gained their demands. It was followed by a general railway strike in the hottest summer for nearly fifty years, and in 1912 by a general strike of miners. The sequence was broken only by the failure of the irresponsible dockers' strike of the same year. It showed the potential strength and weakness of big trade unions, and helped to convert many workers away from the clumsy and wasteful weapon of the general strike towards parliamentary action. Meanwhile each party proposed its own remedy for the distress of the times.

The main answer of the Conservatives was abandonment of free trade; protection against foreign workers and against foreign goods. In 1905 they passed an Aliens Act, designed to restrict the immigration of foreign workers. The number of aliens domiciled in England had more than doubled between 1880 and 1900, and was then nearly one third of a million. A large proportion of the increase were

Jews, recently driven out of eastern Europe, and in London they raised a problem of sweated labour which angered the trade unions. Since the early nineties the Trades Union Congress had demanded limitation on the entry of destitute aliens. The Aliens Act limited entry to eight specified British ports, and gave the government powers of exclusion and even expulsion. Again it was the beginning of future more stringent measures, and it had the support of most of the working-class representatives in Parliament, whether Liberal or Labour. The question of protection against foreign goods raised more political controversy, for it meant a frontal attack on the doctrines of free trade which were the main economic plank of the Liberal platform and a cherished creed among socialists. In 1903 Joseph Chamberlain came out in favour of tariff reform. Having already split the Liberal Party, he now, by adhering to the protectionist wing of the Conservatives, ended by causing a cleavage within the Conservatives. He formed a Tariff Reform League, primarily demanding protection as a unifying force within the Empire, but it merged gradually into an anti-free-trade movement backed by manufacturers who wanted industrial tariffs. It demanded duties on imported food, with preference for the colonies, and an average 10 per cent tariff on foreign manufactured goods. This became the Unionist programme in the elections of 1906, which returned a big Liberal and Labour majority. Conditions were improving by then, and protectionism was declining in popularity. Although tariff reformers were active for the following few years they made no headway before 1914.

The Liberals, competing more effectively than the Conservatives for the electoral support of the working classes, evolved the more popular policy of social reform. Here was something which chimed much more with the real desires of the workers in the strenuously competitive world in which they now found themselves. Protection for individual rights had a more powerful appeal than protection for national industries. Social security was already becoming the key to British politics, and the Liberal and Labour Parties after 1906 combined to satisfy part at least of the new demand. Three measures introduced by the Liberal Governments between 1906 and 1914 deserve special mention. The budget of 1908 provided the sum of £1,200,000 to be set aside for a scheme of old age pensions on a non-contributory basis, to start in 1909. The scale for people over seventy ranged from 1s od to 5s od a week, according to income. An income of 12s od or more a week disqualified anyone from claiming it. Again, it was a modest beginning from which much has followed since. In the next year the Trade Boards Act was passed, to stop 'sweated labour' in certain trades. The Boards were empowered to fix minimum rates of wages, and enforce them, and they worked so well that their scope was soon extended to cover many other trades. In 1911 the National Insurance Act was passed. Part I provided for a vast contributory scheme to insure all the working classes against sickness. The established friendly societies and the trade unions were brought into the scheme as 'approved societies' to administer the monetary benefits to their members. Although it was bitterly opposed by the British Medical Association it resulted in an increase in the nation's supply of doctors and gave the average doctor a higher income. Combined with free medical inspection and treatment of children in schools it went far to raise the national standard of health, and to prevent acute hardship for workers in time of ill-health.[1] Part II of the same Act, as

1. It was not, however, an unmixed blessing: cf. Dr Harry Roberts in *The Nation and Athenaeum*, 1 June 1935: 'When the Insurance Act was introduced the bottle of medicine was just about to settle down on its deathbed. The Act rejuvenated it, and to-day there can hardly be a

already mentioned, provided for contributory unemployment benefits in certain trades.

Taken in bulk the liberal legislation of the period meant that the State had at least accepted it as a duty to promote the welfare of its citizens at the common expense. It had not, by modern standards, pressed this principle very far by 1914, but the principle was accepted. Changes in distributing the burden of taxation reflected it. The budget of 1907 taxed 'unearned' more heavily than 'earned' incomes. The budget of 1909 introduced a 'super-tax' on incomes over £5000, increased death duties, and taxed unearned increment on land-values. By 1913, when government expenditure totalled £200,000,000, about 60 per cent of the revenue came from direct taxation and only 40 per cent from indirect taxes. In 1874 the ratio had been 33 per cent and 67 per cent respectively. In 1913, some £55,000,000 was spent on non-military expenditure: in 1901 less than half that had been spent. Social services, being distributed according to need and not according to work, always act as economically levelling forces. Britain began the present century by squarely facing this principle, and has since followed it out in many of its far-reaching ramifications. In one sense it is but the logical fulfilment of the Benthamite doctrine that the aim of legislation is to promote 'the greatest happiness of the greatest number.' That principle was not inherently connected with doctrines of *laissez-faire*, which happened to be the 'progressive' theories at the time when Bentham wrote. In the course of the century it became divested of such associations, and when changed conditions demanded that it be sought by positive means,

working-class home in the land without a partly consumed eight or ten ounce bottle of bitter or sweet, brown or pinkish mixture, composed of ingredients in the efficacy of which not one doctor in fifty has the slightest faith . . .'

by deliberate social organization and collectivist measures instead of by optimistic trust in an 'invisible hand', the days of *laissez-faire* were numbered; just as when it became clear that British agriculture and industry might not be able to compete with those of foreign countries even on the home market the days of free trade were numbered. The spread of democracy meant that the old purpose, promotion of 'the greatest happiness of the greatest number', should remain the operative ideal of English society, infusing its life with a toleration and a spirit of solidarity which survived even the violent politics of the years before 1914.

It had ceased to be correct to speak only of an 'urban' population. There was also a large and growing 'suburban' population. The nineties saw the coming of the first electric trams, the first 'tubes', and the first motor-cars. By 1914 almost every provincial city of any size had its electric trams, mostly under municipal control, and London had its buses and underground. These changes in urban transport created suburbia. People could live farther from their places of work. There was a building boom in the outskirts of towns. Although the first effect was to relieve some of the congestion in the slums, the eventual result was to attract even more people to the towns, and in the end to swell the town-bred population. Some of the consequences of this new environment on the psychology of the pre-war generation were immense: especially as regards imperial and foreign affairs.

CHAPTER XI

THE NEW IMPERIALISM

The White Man's Burden

A FURTHER consequence of the new balance of power created by the unification of Germany, Italy, and the United States and of their subsequent industrialization was a new and more feverish quest for overseas territories. Colonies came to be valued both as manifestations of national greatness and as sources of raw materials and markets for manufactures. The race for colonies began in the eighties, and in the race Britain and France had certain natural advantages. Both were already advanced in industrialization; both had many overseas possessions. It was Africa which came to be the chief attraction, and between 1870 and 1914 the whole of Africa, apart from one or two small areas, was partitioned among the European powers. The Far East also began to be opened up to the west, and even Pacific islands attracted the new imperialists as naval outposts.

Disraeli had identified the Conservatives with a policy of imperialism. In the interlude between the decline of the Liberal Party and the rise of the Labour Party interest in England tended to concentrate on imperial affairs. From 1895 to 1905 the supremacy of Conservative Governments brought this spirit of imperialism into practical politics. Although England during this decade became in many ways aggressive and 'jingoistic' in foreign and imperial affairs, it was partly because she felt threatened. It was another expression of that consciousness of decline which has already been considered. It was the truculence that came from a great Power, recently so complacent in its greatness, finding itself quite suddenly and through no special shortcomings of its own on the defensive. And it was a mood forcefully embodied in Joseph Chamberlain's policy at the Colonial Office during this decade.

The popular mood of the time is best expressed not so much by the term 'jingoism' as by the group of writers which most appealed to Englishmen at the turn of the century. Robert Louis Stevenson was writing of the adventure and heroism of the South Seas. W. E. Henley from his bed of sickness and pain exalted courage and the glory of living strenuously. The sea attracted them all. Joseph Conrad of the merchant service wrote of the white man in the tropics. Above all Rudyard Kipling, the unofficial spokesman of the new imperialism, wrote of the white man's burden and showed the greatness that might come from struggle and endurance against heavy odds. His creed, if that is not too systematic a word, has been described by that penetrating Frenchman, Élie Halévy, as 'a species of Darwinian philosophy expressed in a mythical form', a 'moral code, chaste, brutal, heroic, and childlike.' He made popular the ideal of a common imperial patriotism, transcending every diversity of birth and circumstance, ennobled by an ideal of selfless service. He has much too often been quoted as an exponent of aggressive imperialism. He is rather the voice of unrepentant but chastened imperialism, seeking perhaps unconsciously to equip British power with a moral purpose and a human content. His most famous poem, 'The Recessional', which he wrote at the conclusion of the Diamond Jubilee, strikes the characteristic note:

> If, drunk with sight of power, we loose
>   Wild tongues that have not thee in awe,
> Such boastings as the Gentiles use,
>   Or lesser breeds without the Law –
> Lord God of Hosts, be with us yet,
> Lest we forget – lest we forget!

It was impressive that the chief bard of imperialism, repelled by the proud self-congratulation of the Jubilee, should feel moved to make this call for humility. His call was little heeded at the time, as the hysteria of Mafeking Night three years later was to show.

The appeal of Kipling, and of a host of much lesser contemporary writers, was especially to a certain section of the new town-bred population: to the newly influential class of black-coated workers, the so-called 'lower-middle' classes, living a drab existence of routine in the towns and suburbs. One of Kipling's favourite themes is the contrast between the adventurous, hard, but heroic life of the British soldier on the frontier or in the lonely station and the unheroic life of his fellow-citizen at home who also is supposed to share in this great Empire. One of his most popular poems, 'Mandalay', concerns the dream of the ex-soldier, longing, amid the dust and drizzle of London, to get back to the spacious spiciness of the East. The more or less educated town and suburban dwellers lived in conditions of semi-gentility and conventional monotony; bank clerks and shop assistants, factory managers and lesser civil servants, armies of them just adjusting themselves to a pinched and colourless existence. Kipling invited them to jump from Streatham to east of Suez, and roam with him the Seven Seas – in imagination. They leapt at the opportunity. By his skilful use of army slang, by his wonderful vocabulary of romantic words and exotic images, by his robust energy verging on the ruffianly, he exerted a strong fascination over the new generation of town-dwellers. Less artistic writers than Kipling catered for similar tastes. The nineties, as Mr Wingfield Stratford has pointed out, were

the decade pre-eminently of magazine supermen, drawn with varying degrees of skill, detectives and criminals, sea captains and banditti, vivified mummies and nondescript mystery men, but all alike in their strength and silence, their practical omnipotence, and omniscience in pursuit of ends often the most trivial. There was the still lower form of standardized melodrama, in which the charms of blonde and submissive virgins are perpetually the reward of blameless fools in conflict with super-subtle villainy (*History of British Civilization*, p. 1171).

The Empire, vividly depicted in the Jubilees and in Kipling, always spreading out red on the map, became the biggest collective adventure of all: even if it had to be enjoyed by proxy.

Sensationalism, the love of excitement without danger, was indeed a characteristic of the spirit of the time in other ways. What the yellow press did for the proletariat, *The Yellow Book* and the other organs of contemporary 'decadence' in literature and art did for the intelligentsia. It is at first sight odd that an Aubrey Beardsley and an Oscar Wilde should flourish in the same atmosphere as a Kipling or a Henley: but the common ground between them was this hunger for sensation. As Mr Holbrook Jackson, in his excellent studies of *The Eighteen Nineties* has suggested, both the 'decadents' and the popular daily press were 'the outcome of a society which had absorbed a bigger idea of life than it knew how to put into practice.' The first half of the decade 'was remarkable for a literary and artistic renaissance, degenerating into decadence; the second for a new sense of patriotism degenerating into jingoism.' The *Daily Mail* and its later imitators openly fanned the flames of jingoism lit by Joseph Chamberlain, Cecil Rhodes, Kipling, and such incidents as the Jameson Raid of 1895, the Fashoda incident of 1898, and Mafeking Night. The 'man-in-the-street' came into his own as the century ended – the product of industrialism-plus-democracy which the twentieth century was to re-christen 'the common man'. If his entry into his political and cultural inheritance was heralded by an outburst of raucous patriotism and a cult of brutal impatience with all resistance to British rule overseas, that was but over-compensation for the utterly unromantic conditions in which his civilization forced him to live. It is significant that two of his favourite writers were Conan Doyle, who brought romance to Baker Street, and G. K. Chesterton, who taught men to see romance in the pillar-box at the corner of the street. The nineties felt 'naughty' mainly because they made a convention of unconventionality.

It was against a background of such developments at home that there took place that long series of colonial conflicts which reached its first phase in the Boer War and its climax in the naval rivalry with Germany and the First World War. War was, indeed, its natural form of expression. In 1878, at the Congress of Berlin, Disraeli had been able to claim that he won 'peace with honour' because Britain had taken no part in the war and yet gained Cyprus out of it for the Empire. In 1898 the clash with France over Fashoda, a remote outpost on the Nile, roused feelings at home to fever-pitch and was ended only when the French, reluctantly but sensibly, gave way. A corresponding quarrel with the Boer farmers of South Africa had simmered on since the time of the Great Trek in 1836. British rule in its expansion northwards from the Cape had pursued them first into Natal and then north of the Orange River. In 1880 the Boers of the Transvaal invaded Natal and defeated the British force at Majuba Hill. A Convention was signed which restored independence to the Transvaal, except for British 'suzerainty' over it. Henceforward the figure of Cecil Rhodes (1853–1902) dominated the African scene. His aim was a united dominion stretching over most of Africa, to be developed jointly by Dutch and British under the British Crown. In East Africa and in the interior of South Africa chartered companies were pressing on in their pioneer advances. The area west of the Transvaal became British in 1885, and the territories to the north (to-day known as Southern and Northern Rhodesia) were taken over. In the nineties Kenya and Uganda became British protectorates. The discovery of gold in the Transvaal attracted a new batch of adventurers, known as 'outlanders', who were refused full citizenship by the Boer government. War broke out between British and Boers in 1899, ostensibly over the grievances of the 'outlanders' but really as the climax to a long story of Kruger's truculent intransigence and of British jostling in her imperial expansion. The chief of the Colonial Office was Joseph Chamberlain (1836–1914), whose aim was certainly to extend and unify the Empire, but whose handling of the situation which led to war has been more and more vindicated against charges of war-mongering as further evidence has come to light. He was the dominating personality in Lord Salisbury's ministry of 1895, and made the Colonial Office unusually important. He found in it the scope for far-reaching plans of development which his restless character demanded, and he ranks as one of the greatest figures in the story of the British Commonwealth.

The chief domestic importance of the war was that it split British public opinion, and especially Liberal opinion, into the pro-war party, including the Conservatives and the Liberal Imperialists led by Lord Rosebery, and the 'pro-Boer' party, led by Lord Morley and Campbell-Bannerman and supported by the Independent Labour Party. The 'pro-Boers' were unpopular at the time, for public opinion on the whole was aggressive, especially in London. But the fact that a large and important section of all classes opposed the war showed a healthy independence of mind which won respect abroad and helped in reconciling the Transvaal seven years later. Lloyd George, above all, made his name as a courageous opponent of the war. The chief international significance of the war was that it invoked great international hostility against Britain and led her to reconsider her old policy of 'splendid isolation'. The initial stages of the war brought heavy defeats which shook complacency in Britain. The later stages were a guerilla warfare in which the Boers excelled and in which they put the overwhelmingly stronger British forces into humiliating positions, and forced them to adopt methods unpopular both at home and abroad. Like the Crimean War, the only other big warlike venture of the period, it revealed great weaknesses in British military organization. It incurred the charge of 'bullying' two small independent States.

Meanwhile great additions to the Empire had been made in other ways. In the eighties British New Guinea, North Borneo, and Upper Burma were added. In 1898, after Kitchener's victories, Anglo-Egyptian control of the Sudan was established. Although France, Germany, Italy, and Belgium added considerable territories to their empires in these years Britain much more than 'held her own'. But, in a way highly characteristic of this whole period, she did so only at very heavy cost. She incurred, perhaps inevitably, the colonial jealousy and naval enmity of Germany. She stirred up considerable hostility in France, which in face of the growing threat of German power to both countries was unnecessary and very short-sighted. She fought, for the first time in half a century, a costly war for which she suffered world-wide odium. But in the end, although the Boer War lasted nearly three years, the cost proved much less than it might have been. If it had revealed to the world unexpected British weaknesses it also revealed them to Britain herself – and Lord Haldane's consequent overhaul of her military organization a few years later was timely. If it further contributed to the splintering of the Liberal Party, it paved the way for a fruitful collaboration between the more radical Liberals and the Labour Party in the years after 1906. Having burnt her fingers once, at a time when memories of the Crimean War were becoming dim, Britain trod more warily during the dangerous years ahead. It has not been possible for even the most ingenious champions of Pan-Germanism to depict the British governments between 1906 and 1914 as reckless or as calculating war-mongers.

Its most immediate effect, as already suggested, was to open the eyes of English leaders – even of Lord Salisbury – to the acute dangers of following a foreign policy of 'splendid isolation' in the new Europe of the twentieth century. If it be assumed that Great Britain would inevitably have become embroiled in the First World War at some stage, it was best she should do so with firm allies with whom certain plans could be concerted beforehand. The Treaty with Japan was signed in the year that the Boer War ended, and the Anglo-French Entente followed two years later. The early defeats of the Boer War shook British self-satisfaction in good time. The generous Peace with which the war ended meant that six years later the three Dutch Premiers of the Transvaal, the Orange Free State, and Cape Colony met the British High Commissioner to draw up a constitution for the new Union of South Africa. The constitution of the Union, which came into force in 1910, was not a federal constitution, as in Canada and Australia. It depended for its working on close cooperation between former enemies. Botha and Smuts virtually ruled the Union, in close sympathy with most of the British residents and of the United Kingdom, until 1918.

Despite the extravagances of much that was said and written in these years about 'the white man's burden', British imperialism even in this, its most dynamic and aggressive phase, was never racialist. Other contemporary imperialisms were racialist. 'Pan-Germanism' had strong racialist elements; 'Pan-Slavism', when it was not a mere device for Russian expansionism, meant solidarity of Slav peoples against Teutonic; 'Pan-Turanianism' meant union of all peoples of Turkish stock. Only 'Pan-Americanism', which also dates from 1889, involved, like the British Commonwealth, free and voluntary cooperation between States with certain affinities and common interests, regardless of race. In spite, too, of the various schemes that were canvassed during these years for closer federation of the Commonwealth, steps were actually taken towards making the association between Dominions and the United Kingdom more openly voluntary in character. Colonial Conferences were held (mostly in London) in 1887, 1894, 1897, 1902, 1907, and 1911. At the fifth Conference the seven Premiers passed a resolution to meet every four years and substituted the term 'Dominions' for that of 'Colonies' to describe the self-governing territories of the empire. A proposal for a permanent Imperial Council was defeated, and it was decided that each government should be left free to settle its own system of tariffs. Consultation remained the only function of imperial conferences, but at least the Dominions Premiers got to know and trust one another, and such understanding proved useful in the crisis of 1914.

The shadow haunting the twenty-five years before 1914 was the shadow of war. In conditions of jealous national and imperial rivalries the most trivial incidents served to start a scare of war. It is remarkable how States, actually so little prepared for war, were so ready to talk lightly of going to war. Nearly every year from 1895 onwards brought war or a scare of war. Just as the United Kingdom engaged so light-heartedly in war against the Boers, so the United States embarked gaily on her war against Spain in 1898. Each lost more lives through disease and mismanagement than through direct enemy action. In 1895 war was even threatened between Britain and the United States. It was a period of amazing swaggering. On music-hall stages leading comedians and leading ladies swaggered and led choruses of swaggering songs about 'Soldiers of the Queen'. In the nineties the epidemic-song, a new phenomenon, was 'Ta-ra-ra-boom-de-ay'. The Germans goose-stepped their way towards military aggression. Statesmen, American, German, or British, on the slightest provocation or with none at all, rattled their sabres. The careless optimism with which masses of people were able to contemplate a major European war served only to indicate their ignorance of what it would be like with the modern resources of scientific warfare. The climax of a century of expanding political democracy, in France and America and Britain, was a new level of hysteria and irresponsibility in politics. So much talk of war, made ever more real by the tightening system of alliances by which each great Power was more helplessly bound to its allies, led inevitably to the building of vast national armaments. To examine the historical consequences of this new kind of 'international anarchy', we must turn to the leading international developments, so far as Great Britain was concerned, of the decades between 1874 and 1914.

The Drift towards War

Before the Boer War, although Bismarck and his successors had been building up a system of great alliances in Europe designed, at first, to keep the peace by a subtle and intricately manipulated balance of power, Britain had managed to keep out of entanglements. Her official foreign policy, of keeping a free hand and preserving a position of 'splendid isolation', worked well until the Boer War. It rested on the fact that she distrusted France almost as much as she distrusted Germany, and continued to fear Russian expansion more than either. Her experience of universal animosity during the Boer War, coupled with the initial reverses and subsequent humiliations which she suffered at the hands of the Boer guerrilla fighters, made her feel dangerously friendless in a world where no great Power could afford to be friendless. The first treaty of the Triple Alliance between Germany, Austria, and Italy was made in 1882; it was clearly aimed at Russia in the east and at France in the west. By 1894 France and Russia, faced with this common danger, drew together and made a military convention and alliance. German support for Kruger and the Boers, symbolized by the Kaiser's telegram to Kruger in 1896 congratulating him on the repulse of the Jameson Raid, and the later activities of the Kaiser and von Tirpitz in preparing naval armaments, combined to scare Britain into thoughts of an *entente* with France. In 1902 she made an alliance with Japan – the first clear sign that isolationism was dead. Two years later she reached an *entente* with France. It was not a military or even a naval alliance. It was mainly a removal of colonial disputes between the two countries, arranging roughly that in return for British hegemony in Egypt France gained hegemony in Morocco. German efforts to disrupt it only hammered it firmer, and three years later the Triple Entente was completed by an agreement between Britain and Russia. Europe was now divided into two rival armed camps, and any dispute anywhere had immediate repercussions and formidable implications for every great Power. Whilst Germany bewailed 'encirclement' Britain regarded every new step in Germany's naval programme as aimed at her own naval supremacy, and reacted accordingly. The vicious circle of suspicion breeding suspicion began to dominate all else.

From 1908 onwards Britain's attitude, both official and popular, towards Germany was determined mainly by the naval problem. It reached the level of panic in March, 1909, when a writer in *The Times* declared, 'The people will be quite sane in a fortnight – they always went like this in March.' Sir John Fisher, in process of a great technical overhaul of British naval strength, launched his first Dreadnought in 1905. Germany planned a building programme which would give her thirteen capital ships – battleships and armoured cruisers – by 1912. A split developed within the British Cabinet between those who argued that to build four more would give Britain a safe margin in three years' time, and those who demanded six. The division was bridged by a compromise that four be authorized and four more be laid down if developments in Germany seemed to warrant it. As Winston Churchill, who supported only four, later wrote, 'The Admiralty had demanded six: the economists offered four: and we finally compromised on eight.' Discussion of the whole matter in Parliament and the press became exaggerated and distorted, and it became a party issue. The Conservatives and the Navy League took up the slogan 'We want eight and we won't wait.' The hysteria did not die down in a fortnight – it lasted into the summer – and historians have put forward widely varying interpretations of why it reached such heights and lasted so long. Was it due to a plot of arms manufacturers and black reactionaries, for certainly the big armaments firms took some hand in working up the panic? Was it a mere by-product of the parliamentary and party system, which required any government engaged in an armaments programme to justify its financial costs by rousing public opinion? Or was it a result of the strain and psychological tensions in national opinion, an abnormal reaction after the abnormal self-confidence and cocksureness of the earlier decades? All three factors seem to have combined in a disastrous way.[1] Yet it was followed by strenuous efforts to reach compromise and conciliation with Germany.

In 1912 Lord Haldane was sent to Berlin to explore terms. But the Germans insisted on a political equivalent for any concessions on their part, and that equivalent seemed to be detachment of Britain from France and Russia; or at least a pledge of British neutrality should Germany become involved in war, which would amount in effect to the same thing. British proposals for 'a naval holiday' were regarded as a trap. Any form of disarmament was out of the question when international fears were so great. In the same year Sir Edward Grey, the British Foreign Secretary, was instructed to exchange letters with M. Cambon of France in order to make clear to France the exact limitations of British commitments. Since the making of the *entente* British naval strength in the Mediterranean had been decreased and transferred to the Atlantic and the North Sea. Britain now gave up first-line responsibility to the French in the Mediterranean, and assumed it in the Atlantic and the Channel. There was no formal alliance even now, but this distribution of functions in defence linked the policy of the two countries more intimately than any formal treaty could ever have done. The Grey-Cambon correspondence noted that 'the disposition of the French and British fleets respectively at the present moment is not based upon an engagement to cooperate in war.' Facts were to prove stronger than lack of words: and the same letter actually engaged both governments to consult should war threaten either. The steady pressure of Anglo-German relations was towards naval rivalry, and that

1. cf. for these three views P. Noel-Baker: *The Private Manufacture of Armaments*, Vol. I (1936); O. J. Hale: *Publicity and Diplomacy, 1890–1914* (1940); C. E. Playne: *The Pre-War Mind in Britain* (1928). And see E. L. Woodward: *Great Britain and the German Navy* (1935).

of Anglo-French relations was towards naval cooperation. These facts remained inescapable until the end.

Between 1912 and 1914 there were two Balkan Wars, involving Turkey directly and both Russia and Austria-Hungary by implication. The Slav State of Serbia was backed by Russia in her bitter struggle against Austria-Hungary. Strenuous efforts of the other Powers to prevent these Balkan conflicts from spreading into a general European war succeeded. But in the end it was the murder of an Austrian Archduke by a Serbian extremist at Sarajevo which precipitated the world war. The situation has been well summarized by Mr J. A. Spender:

> The stage which Europe had reached was that of a semi-inter-nationalism which organized the nations into two groups but provided no bridge between them. There could scarcely have been worse conditions for either peace or war. The equilibrium was so delicate that a puff of wind might destroy it, and the immense forces on either side were so evenly balanced that a struggle between them was bound to be stupendous. The very success of the balance of power was in this respect its nemesis. (*Fifty Years of Europe*, p. 389.)

The truth was that the two historic empires of Turkey and Austria-Hungary were rapidly disintegrating. The defeat of Turkey by the Balkan States gave impetus to a process which was bound to lead to upheaval. Mutual fears of Russia and Austria-Hungary meant their rivalry for pickings in the disintegrating Turkish empire. Germany's fears of encirclement meant that she dared not desert Austria-Hungary, now intent on demolishing the rising power of Serbia which was threatening her own imperial existence. France, terrified of Germany, dared not desert Russia which was willing to back Serbia. So the chains of the alliance system, in a world filled with fear, pulled one nation after another into the entanglement. Until the very end, despite all the indications already given, the issue of British participation remained unsettled. It is most improbable, in view of her naval arrangements with France and her inevitable concern for the balance of power in Europe, that Britain could for long have kept out of a war which involved the other partners in the alliances. The issue which made her immediate participation inevitable was the German invasion of Belgium, dictated by Germany's adoption of the Schlieffen plan of campaign in 1914. By the Treaty of 1838 Britain, like France, was a guarantor of Belgian neutrality, though she had not in all circumstances an obligation to defend it. Gladstone in 1870 had strengthened the guarantees of neutrality, and it was a traditional element in British defensive policy to prevent the Low Countries from falling into the hands of a great rival continental Power. By 3 August 1914 Austria was at war with Serbia, Germany was at war with Russia and with France. When Germany, on the morning of the 4th, invaded Belgium and the Belgian King appealed to Britain for aid, Britain declared war on Germany that day.

Before war was declared each Dominion Government assured the United Kingdom of its support. Canada, Australia, and New Zealand sent volunteer armies, the Union of South Africa suppressed a rebellion of irreconcilables and proceeded to invade German South-West Africa. Redmond brought in the Irish voluntarily. In the end Germany had to fight one and a quarter million men from the Dominions. The British Commonwealth remained a unity in the time of test.

The Issues at Stake

What, in the light of previous history, was the war of 1914 about? At the time it was said that Britain entered the war in fulfilment of her treaty obligations to defend Belgium's neutrality and in defence of the sanctity of treaties which the German Chancellor described as 'scraps of paper'. Behind this reason, which certainly did much to determine both the unanimity and the timing of Britain's declaration of war, lay the deep-rooted historical tradition of her foreign policy which resisted all attempts of other great Powers to dominate the Low Countries and the approaches of the North Sea. It can equally be argued that just as strong a tradition was her concern for the safety of the Channel ports and anxiety to preserve either a weak or a friendly Power across the Channel. For this reason, too, Britain was unlikely to permit passively German occupation of France: and it was recognition of this fact which had made her enter into arrangements which dovetailed her own naval dispositions with those of France. It is a remarkable fact that, just as the outbreak of war was prefaced by more than two years of repeated efforts on the part of Britain to reach understanding with Germany, so until the actual outbreak of war there was little passion, hatred, or malice displayed in the press of either country. In this final phase they showed considerable understanding of one another's point of view. The issues which had aroused so much excitement in the past did not figure at all in the publicity of either country. We must be careful not to underestimate the actual share of both her Belgian and French commitments in bringing Britain into the war, and to exaggerate her economic and colonial rivalries with Germany.

Behind the decisions in 1914 lay more than a quarter-century of rivalry in power between Britain and the great imperial States of Europe; of periodic war-scares and crises; of feverish competition in armaments; of nervous tensions and anxieties. The previous decade, especially, after the making of the Anglo-French *entente*, had been one of intensive propaganda over naval competition with Germany, trade rivalry, espionage, scares of invasion.[1] The full effects of the new balance of power created by 1870 had been working themselves out. The political upheavals produced by the break-up of the Turkish and Austro-Hungarian empires would have yielded material enough for a hundred international frictions, even apart from the age-old hatreds between France and Germany and traditional British anxieties about the balance of power in the west. The participation of Britain in the World War, viewed in its longest perspective, was the inevitable consequence of her worldwide supremacy, both economic and naval, during the mid-Victorian era: for that supremacy was something she was losing, but which she would not be likely to bring herself to accept as lost without a struggle to retain it. That is where the naval challenge of Germany became so important.

The Belgian issue silenced opposition to a war policy among Liberals and Labour. Regarding war as in itself immoral, they had to support it in the name of a new morality. On the day that war was declared, Mr J. L. Garvin in the *Pall Mall Gazette* wrote:

> We have to do our part in killing a creed of war. Then at last, after a rain of blood, there may be set the greater rainbow in the Heavens before the vision of the souls of men. And after Armageddon war, indeed, may be no more.

The idea of a 'war to end war', and linked with it the ideal of a 'war to make the world safe for democracy', grew in strength as the war progressed. As the alignment of Powers changed – as Italy joined the western democracies, Russia dropped out of the camp of the allies, and the United States came in – this ideological purpose gained in strength. In

1. Including even fantastic scares, such as the airship panic of 1913 based on mythical airships seen over the British coast by many 'eye-witnesses'. The 'flying saucers' after the Second World War are the contemporary counterpart.

germ, at least, it was there from the first among the Liberals and Radicals and Socialists who supported Grey over the Belgian issue. In all the many issues at stake in the war – and only those directly affecting Britain have been mentioned here – the war was historically the culmination of the nineteenth century. It marked the end of an epoch even if, unhappily, it did not prove to mark the beginning of another of the kind for which its sufferers hoped.

CHAPTER XII

VICTORIAN ENGLAND IN RETROSPECT

The Three Phases of Victorianism

IF the terms 'Victorian' or 'nineteenth-century' England be stretched to include the historical period between the end of the great French Wars and the beginning of the First World War, what generalizations can be made about its development and its characteristics? First, and most obviously, it was a period of extraordinary peace. The seventeenth century had been a period of civil war and revolutions; the eighteenth a period of recurrent wars, usually against France. In Europe the nineteenth century, too, appears as outstandingly a period of recurrent revolutions and big wars. In English history it has a quite different, and indeed unique, character. The only two wars of any importance in which Britain found herself embroiled, the Crimean War and the Boer War, are alike in the recklessness and irresponsibility with which they were undertaken and the unnecessary high toll of losses which they exacted; but in other ways they differ. The Crimean War was waged against a major Power historically distrusted by Britain and was an attempt to check that Power's expansion. It was waged in company with France – the traditional enemy – and with strong support elsewhere in Europe. The Boer War was waged against two small farmers' republics, and was occasioned by Britain's own expansion colonially. It was waged without allies and amid the general hostility of all Europe. Neither engagement could ever have developed into a prolonged major conflict between the greatest European Powers. Relatively it was, for Britain, a period of conspicuous peace.

Moreover, the period is equally conspicuously one which is bounded by two momentous wars, and this fact gives it its three-fold shape. From 1815 to about 1850 the effects of the French Revolution, the Empire of Napoleon and the French Wars were working themselves out. Their effects were more direct and more profound in Europe than in Britain, which partly explains her relative immunity from revolution and war during this first period. But even in Britain the forces of democratic radicalism, born of the American and French Revolutions at the end of the eighteenth century, were in ferment and were influencing the growth of her whole political and constitutional system. More important, by reason of a happy conjunction of circumstances which included her rapid growth in population, her large natural resources of coal, and her native inventiveness, industrialization proceeded apace while other countries more tormented by the aftermath of the wars and the ideals of the Revolution, were retarded in their economic growth. Undergoing a prolonged industrial revolution at the same time as she was carrying out moderate and gradual political reforms, Britain attained double pre-eminence in the world as a model of constitutional government and as a producer of cheap manufactured goods. The overflowing of her surplus population into the uncolonized territories of the world also laid a basis for her later Commonwealth, peopled mainly by folk of British stock. For these reasons the years around the middle of the nineteenth century mark the climax of British power, prestige, and prosperity.

Finally, during the last quarter of the nineteenth century, the various component elements of British pre-eminence, which by coming together during the middle decades had raised her to a unique supremacy in the world, began to fall apart and to be destroyed. Her increase in population slowed down, for her birth-rate began to decline after 1870, her industrial and commercial strength no longer went unchallenged, the balance of international power upon which she had relied to give her an easy national security was completely altered, and even her naval supremacy began to be questioned by the United States on one hand and by Germany on the other. Although she continued to the end to add extensively to her overseas territories, and to evolve a political framework within which the British Dominions overseas remained in free but close cooperation and loyalty to her, she became increasingly aware that the era of her easy supremacy was approaching its end. Viewed in retrospect, the generation before 1914 was as much a 'pre-war generation' as that after 1815 had been a 'post-war generation'. If one had had to grapple with the problems bequeathed by an era of great upheaval and war, the other had to deal with the issues which were creating an era of further great upheaval and war.

It is therefore not artificial to see the Victorian age as falling into three main phases, differentiated broadly by three successive generations. When the conditions of human environment are changing very fast each rising generation has to tackle fresh problems, effect novel self-adjustments of outlook and habit, discover how to adapt old institutions and invent new ones, without very much guidance from past experience. What distinguishes the mid-Victorian generation from its predecessor and its successor is its prevailing belief that it had solved satisfactorily so many of its problems: though even here, as has been shown, contemporary critics were never more active and seldom more corrosive in their criticisms.

Taken together, as phases of one continuous process, the

adjustments and responses of the three generations of the nineteenth century amount to a very remarkable achievement. By 1914, as compared with 1815, men and women in Britain were much more numerous, more long-lived, better fed, better clothed, better housed, more healthy, more literate, better informed, more keenly interested in social and international affairs, better governed, more mobile, more scientific in outlook, better equipped with resources of producing wealth, and better supplied with every sort of social amenity. If they were vastly more healthy and more wealthy, were they also more wise? That is impossible to answer. Certainly they were more gregarious in their habits, less religious in their outlook, more prone to mass hysteria and sensationalism, more dependent on what happened everywhere else on earth, than their great-grandfathers had been. They had abolished or diminished many age-long evils – the sin of slavery, the crime of ruthless exploitation, the distress of destitution, the plague of epidemics, the ills of bigotry and ignorance. But in spite of so much visible 'progress' and 'improvement', other mighty evils had descended upon them: the drab squalor of mining and industrial cities, the ravages of the countryside, the menace of mass unemployment, the terror of economic crisis, and the frightfulness of scientific war. No balance-sheet can be drawn up when the assets and liabilities are so tremendous. But the process by which they were accumulated and incurred deserves study.

Strength through Liberalism

The three phases of Victorian development coincide respectively with the growth, supremacy, and decline of Liberalism as the operative political creed of most Englishmen. Is there therefore any connexion between Liberalism and Victorian greatness? Élie Halévy, in his volume of *The Age of Peel and Cobden*, suggests that there was, at least, a connexion between Liberalism and the national solidity of British life and institutions in the middle phase.

> British Liberalism, that is to say, was regarded by the English themselves as intimately bound up with the solidity of their institutions. Was Liberalism a result of the solidity, or the solidity of the institutions?
>
> The English were inclined to accept the latter explanation... One thing alone was certain. The formation of parties in Parliament, of public opinion in the country, was polarized by the ideal of freedom.

Mr Gladstone believed, and practised the belief, that

> methodically to enlist the members of a community, with due regard to their several capacities, in the performance of its public duties, is the way to make that community powerful and healthful, to give a firm seat to its rulers, and to engender a warm and intelligent devotion to those beneath their sway.

It is as true to say that Liberalism was a result of the solidity as that it produced the solidity. The ideal of freedom, for individuals, groups, and the national community alike, had already deep roots in English development. The permanent motivating ideal of nineteenth-century England in its legislation and successive reforms was 'the greatest happiness of the greatest number.' That novel ideal was Radical and democratic, and sprang from the rationalist, humanitarian thought of the eighteenth century. Though it came to be closely associated with English Liberalism it had no intrinsic or inevitable connexion with it. Through its associations with the other teachings of Adam Smith and Jeremy Bentham, and through its connexions with English Liberalism, it came to be linked with a very negative view of the State and its role in the community. The doctrines of *laissez-faire* were adopted with enthusiasm by nineteenth-century England because they were so admirably suited to a period of rapid expansion. During the first generation of the century, when the chief aim was emancipation from old restrictions and encumbrances, it seemed natural and logical, after demanding freedom of thought and speech and religious worship, to go on to demand freedom of enterprise, free competition, free markets, and free trade. So long as maximum production was the end and the speediest exploitation of resources the means, in a rapidly growing community with expanding means of production at its disposal, it seemed completely true that free individual enterprise was best. Protection of national industries or of overseas trade was utterly unnecessary. Likewise, given so great a national lead over possible rivals, free trade was in the common interest. Liberalism, by the middle of the century, came to mean the completest individual freedom for every citizen who could contribute to the national wealth.

At this point its commercial and political principles were expanded and elaborated into a general philosophy of life. Because national industries needed no protection it was too easily assumed that the individual citizen, in his economic life, needed no protection. Because the British navy was supreme on the seas, it was even assumed that the nation needed no other protection. Because the City of London in fact controlled the financial system of the world, it was assumed that national currency and finance needed no other protection. Similarly, truth itself needed no better guarantee than the constant free play of criticism and discussion. This was Mill's argument in his essay *On Liberty:* or, as the epitome of the period, Lord Palmerston, put it a dozen years earlier than Mill:

> It is by comparing opinions – by a collision of opinions – by rubbing one man's opinions against those of another and seeing which are the hardest and will bear the friction best – that men, in or out of office, can most justly arrive at the knowledge of what is most advantageous to the interests of the whole community.

The progressive extensions of the vote, the working of the parliamentary party system, the whole texture of representative constitutional government, made sense only if it were assumed that every man is not only entitled to have opinions but actually has opinions; that these opinions, sturdily held and respected, are worth having and hearing; and that 'knowledge of what is most advantageous to the interests of the whole community' will be discovered by taking into account what people want as well as what the experts pronounce it to be good that they should have. The free competition of ideas and opinions, and free enterprise in propounding and discussing them – that was the essence of intellectual Liberalism. It provided an environment in which scientific enquiry and discovery made amazingly rapid progress: and the consequence of free thought was free thinking. Bradlaugh and the Rationalist Press Association were the natural concomitants of Charles Darwin and T. H. Huxley.

In this way Liberalism, as a creed, had its roots directly in the principles of *laissez-faire*. The triumph of free trade and of Cobdenism identified it henceforth with commercial *laissez-faire* and also, by simple transference, with resistance to more than a minimum of governmental interference with social and economic life in domestic affairs. These beliefs of Liberalism were beliefs about means rather than about ends. They indicated how certain things could best be attained, without specifying very carefully what these things should be. The ends of maximum production in economics, of individual freedom in politics, of free association in society, were assumed rather than considered. They stood unquestioned, for a time, as the obvious *desiderata* of mid-Victorian Britain. The steadiness of purpose which underlay all Liberal reforms of the period came really from the Radical goal – the promotion of 'the greatest happiness of the greatest number.' That is why the most striking advances in providing greater security for the individual citizen – the Factory Acts and the organization of public health – came not from Liberalism itself but from either above or below middle-class Liberalism: from Tory philanthropy or Tory Radicalism, from Radicalism or trade unionism. The negative character of mid-Victorian Liberalism was made possible partly because forces outside itself provided more positive criteria of action and more positive values, partly because so long as material and physical expansion continued the ever-receding horizon drew men on to fresh efforts without the goal being too clearly defined.

It all worked well so long as the sky was the limit. It was when these conditions changed and became less favourable that the time for heart-searching and questioning began. When national capacity for exporting became more restricted, when Britain's lead over others shortened, when her prospects of further expansion contracted and her supremacy was challenged, then did Liberalism begin to decline. The root of the trouble was that its old implicit ends were no longer enough; and not being clearly formulated or appreciated, it was some time before they were seen to be not enough. It was not enough to go on producing the greatest possible amount of wealth unless you decided what to do with the wealth when you had got it. It was not enough to give all men political and economic freedom unless they had worthy ways in which to use that freedom. It was not enough to pay homage to all opinions unless most of those opinions were worthy of respect. The history of latter-day Victorian Liberalism was, in fine, the quest for a new morality, a new and more adequate set of moral values. It prolonged its life well into the twentieth century because it to some extent found such values. The moral Liberalism of Campbell-Bannerman, Lloyd George, and the 'pro-Boers', the social

Liberalism which put through the sequence of much-needed reforms extending social welfare and security between 1906 and 1914, the Liberal Imperialism which evolved Dominion status and did so much to health wounds in South Africa: these were the life-blood of latter-day Liberalism. But by then it had breathed life into new movements which, under other names such as Fabianism, trade unionism, and Socialism, carried the same moral values more generously and actively into social life, and pursued the new social purpose of fairer distribution of wealth, rating welfare above wealth and security above prestige.

The moral fibre which sustained mid-Victorian Britain in its era of greatness was derived only partly from the moral values of Liberalism. This can be seen by glancing at the typical mid-Victorian virtues which a strong family life and a powerful social opinion favoured against all others. Industriousness, tolerance, self-reliance and self-help, earnest endeavour, liberality of mind: these came mainly from Liberalism, and were the characteristic virtues of a successful business middle-class. Piety, fidelity to the pledged word, good faith in human relationships, charity: these came rather from the deep religious convictions of mid-Victorian England, from its evangelicalism, its fear of an after-life, its Protestant Christianity. Latterly the advance of scientific knowledge, or free-thinking, of aggressive nationalism all contributed to undermine these virtues: and when they declined so too did the characteristic virtues of Liberalism. Much of Matthew Arnold's analysis and criticism was true. The evils of philistinism, smugness, bad taste, and jingoism were there from the first: it was when they ceased to be restrained and offset by the practice of the Christian virtues that the moral rot set in, and with it the decline of Liberal England. Ultimately this decline was a moral collapse: though how far it was due to a moral collapse, or how far this collapse was itself due to the passing of the essential material conditions of British supremacy, is a philosophical problem beyond the judgement of the historian. It is his job to describe and explain the process, so far as he can, by which this double decline came to pass: that has been the chief aim of this book.

In addition to the moral fibre which suffered this change, two other factors come into the picture. One is the deep underlying national unity of Britain in these years. At an historically earlier stage than any other country, except perhaps France and Switzerland, the British Isles had attained real national unification. England since the time of the Norman Conquest, Wales since the time of the Tudors, Scotland since the reign of Queen Anne, had become merged more and more into one unified kingdom, with a common political system and a common way of life. Despite the new and very important internal social divisions and conflicts of group interests which existed in the nineteenth century (and which were examined above in Chapter II), a real sense of community in nationhood remained throughout stronger than in most other European countries. This transcendent spirit of nationality is a constant and vital factor in nineteenth-century British history. Closely linked with it, and in part an explanation of it, is the second factor: the existence of equally well-rooted and flexible institutions of government and of social life. The monarchy, the parliamentary system, the Church and the nonconformist bodies, the communities of town and countryside, the legal system, the Bank of England, the Universities: all had attained great stability in the course of the eighteenth century without losing their adaptability and flexibility. Even amidst the most rapid and ramified of changes in the nineteenth century these institutions of national life could be preserved, adjusted, modified, and used for new ends. They provided a core of stability, continuity, and homogeneity which preserved the identity of the nation.

It is significant that in the last generation of the nineteenth century this core of continuity, too, came to be challenged. The least homogeneous national element in Great Britain, Ireland, erupted in a demand for Home Rule and eventually for total separation. The greatest failure of Victorian statecraft came home to roost in the movement of Sinn Fein, and for a generation it threw British politics into confusion. At the same time separatist forces appeared in the whole 'Celtic fringe', in Wales and even in Scotland, as well as in Ireland. The eighties saw a movement to introduce bilingual teaching into Welsh schools and revive Welsh language and literature; the nineties an attempted Celtic revival in Scotland led by William Sharp ('Fiona Macleod') and Patrick Geddes; and the whole generation saw a major Celtic renaissance in Ireland which gave fame to the names of W. B. Yeats, Douglas Hyde, Lady Gregory, George Russell, J. M. Synge, and G. B. Shaw. Before long weak Home Rule movements appeared in Wales and Scotland, though neither made much progress. Under Gladstone and until 1914 the Liberal Party came to rely more and more upon radical support from this Celtic fringe. The basis of its reliance was Gladstone's famous 'Newcastle Programme' of 1891, which included Irish Home Rule, church disestablishment in Wales and Scotland, and a local veto on the sale of alcohol (this to please the puritanism of the chapels). Except in the landslide election of 1906, when social reform won the day, the Liberal Party never again after this date won a majority in England. It was driven on to the political as well as the geographical periphery of British politics, and died amid what Tennyson would have called 'the blind hysterics of the Celt'.

The Philosophy of the Nineteenth Century

If we turn from the story of the implicit political thought of the period to the more explicit schools of political philosophy it appears that there is a striking parallel between them. The early period, with its profound faith in a natural and automatic harmony of interests between individuals and between nations, has its philosophical counterpart in the reign of the utilitarian Radicalism of the early Benthamites, in the optimistic philanthropic socialism of Robert Owen, in the aristocratic creed of *noblesse oblige* of Lord Shaftesbury. In the flush of victorious nationalism after the great French Wars it seemed so obvious that Britain was one community that it was in no way stupid to speak of there being a natural harmony of interests among her citizens. If there was poverty, private philanthropy and charity would alleviate it; if there was sweated labour in mine or mill, mild legislative restrictions would remedy that; if agricultural and industrial interests seemed at cross-purposes, free discussion coupled with the removal of old and burdensome restrictions would smooth out these conflicts; if there were harsh penal laws, they could be gradually and carefully reformed. The full scale and scope of the great transformation that was taking place was not appreciated by more than a few voices crying in the wilderness until a decade after Queen Victoria came to the throne. Bentham nurtured his belief in an automatic harmony of interests by paying it full homage in economic theory but leaving some room, however restricted, for positive legislation to create an 'artificial' harmony in political and legal affairs. But enlightened self-interest, given free play, would solve all. Owen believed that by openly substituting cooperation for competition, by a change of habits and of heart, men might leap in one bound from the old order into the 'New Harmony': and this belief, coupled with that in the efficacy of paternalist management, he only latterly and reluctantly gave up. Shaftesbury wanted timely and generous humanitarian reforms, effected by the aristocracy, to reconcile them with the new working class: given this, harmony would result and national unity be preserved. The thought of the period is all of a piece.

In the middle phase this optimism spread and was applied by Cobden and Bright to international affairs, by the disciples of Durham to colonial affairs. Free trade would bring a natural division of labour among the nations as well as maximum wealth for all: with prosperity would come a natural harmony and world peace. In a freely self-governing empire cooperation would bring unity. But at the same time an opposite theory of inherent and even 'natural' conflict began to be propounded. While Disraeli spoke of 'the two nations' Marx wrote of the class war. While Carlyle pressed the urgency of the 'condition of England question' and the division between 'Dandies and Drudges', Darwin explained the struggle for survival and the process of evolution by which only the fittest naturally survived. It seemed every bit as true to say that there was a natural conflict of interest as to say that there was a natural harmony of interest, between individuals, groups, or national communities. The Hegelian dialectic seemed to be visibly at work, and antithesis had followed thesis, though none could yet see the synthesis.

But to express it like this is to mislead by oversimplification. The notion of progress through conflict to harmony was there from the start. Even in the first phase the favourite notion was one of collision – collision of individual interests, opinions, wills. And even in the middle phase the culmination of conflict was harmony – the Tory-Democracy of Disraeli, the classless society of Marx, the balance of nature of Darwin, the rule of the superman of Carlyle. The difference was fundamentally one of emphasis rather than of contradiction: and it is in this sense that nineteenth-century philosophy forms one corpus of thought with peculiar and characteristic features of its own. The get-together geniality of Dickens, the cultural homogeneity yearned for by Matthew Arnold, the 'parliament of man, the federation of the world' foreseen by Tennyson, belong to this same body of thought. It was still a picture of unity transcending diversity.

So too, in the third phase which came to be called 'decadence', the same set of ideas survived but with differing degrees of emphasis. But the emphasis was now more strongly on diversity and conflict, more weakly on unity and harmony. Unity was sought in the vaguer, more unreal entities of race and of empire. Men thought more in Nietzschean terms of 'the will to power'. The collision of ideas, rapidly becoming a clash of ideologies, took concrete shape in the new movements of violence: in the violence of the Irish independence movement, the suffragette movement, the trade union movement, the Boer War, and the new imperialisms, eventually the consummation of all in the World War itself. With increasing use of obstruction, crime, strikes, sabotage, and open war as political methods the Liberal faith and practice of constitutionalism were undermined. But political philosophers were busy re-interpreting these developments in the conventional terms of nineteenth-century thought. The idealist philosophers, T. H. Green and Bernard Bosanquet, found in refinements of the idea of a 'general will' a method of harmonising, in theory, the 'real will' of the individual with the law and government of the State. Sidney Webb and the Fabians found in the doctrine of 'the inevitability of gradualness' a device which, they hoped and believed, would reconcile with existing institutions the demands of the new labouring classes. Socialists, of diverse brands, looked forward to a commonwealth wherein co-operatives, trade unions, or industrial guilds would achieve harmony through a socialist reorganization of society.

The philosophical counterparts to the achievements of the yellow press and the more preciously 'sensational' *Yellow Book* were the new group of social psychologists, like Graham Wallas and William McDougall, who probed the irrational forces in human nature, ranging from the instincts of man to the working of his subconscious, which condition the conduct of man in society. Amidst the experience of how the newly emancipated and enfranchized masses could behave, these writers promoted a general questioning of the aridly rationalistic and individualistic assumptions of old Liberalism and Radicalism. The very nature of 'public opinion' and how it is made came to be questioned, and with it the meaning and validity of representative democracy. Like the events of the last phase these writers raised more questions than they answered and more doubts than they allayed. Harmony, if ever there was to be such a thing, was relegated to the realm of the mysterious and the unknowable, if not yet the unattainable. The clash of surrounding nationalisms and rival imperialisms threw public opinion and its theorists back nakedly upon the old core of homogeneity which had preceded Liberalism and its accompanying doctrines, the core of simple national solidarity and national unity. The Socialists who resisted the outbreak of war in 1914 were influential but few, and pacifists were at most a despised and persecuted minority.

The related ideas of harmony and conflict haunted nearly all English nineteenth-century thought in a manner peculiarly its own. It was the doctrines and practice of Liberalism that gave these ideas their peculiar nineteenth-century flavour. The decline of Liberalism was more than the decline of a particular political party. It marked the passing of an epoch, with the habits and ways of thinking peculiar to that epoch. The residue that it left behind was extremely important and extremely valuable. It left a great legacy of experience in free constitutional government, a nation cleared of many old evils, a luminous example of liberality in politics. Its chief heirs, the radical, socialist, and labour movements of the twentieth century, were made distinct from corresponding movements in other countries by the strong flavour of Liberalism they retained. So too was English conservatism, whose readiness to reform is so different from foreign conservatisms. The spirit of Victorian Liberalism remained diffused throughout not only English society but also throughout the whole framework of the British Commonwealth.

It cannot, however, be said that in Britain 'its soul goes marching on'; because in Britain the conditions which had given it birth and which were essential to its survival were rapidly passing away. There is a sense in which by some transmigration of souls it crossed the Atlantic, where conditions of expansion were still congenial to it. It reached its authentic climax in 1919 not with Lloyd George but in Woodrow Wilson. The shades of Cobden and Palmerston would have bowed in familiar recognition of the Fourteen Points, and Mr Gladstone at least might have been prepared to sign the Covenant of the League. But though the first two of Franklin Roosevelt's 'Four Freedoms' – freedom of expression and freedom of worship – are in the direct lineage, the other two – freedom from want and freedom from fear – belong to the spirit of our own times.

Envoi

If the age of Liberalism has passed, what has taken its place? A full answer to that is still impossible, and anyhow goes far beyond the province of this book. One clear element is that 'reform' has given place to 'reconstruction'. Had Britain not been engaged in major wars before 1815 a programme of reforms would still have been necessary during the first generation of the nineteenth century. The agrarian and industrial revolutions made an overhaul of the governmental and economic systems inevitable. Likewise, had war by some miracle been averted in 1914, a period of reconstruction would have become essential by 1919. The rise of the urban, industrial workers to political power and to a new degree of organization made a new kind of demand on society and the State.' Freedom from want and freedom from fear, which are but another way of writing social security, demanded different kinds of social and economic organization from those which had been evolved by nineteenth-century Liberalism. They belong peculiarly to the world of crisis, contraction, and organized violence which is the twentieth century. They require, for their fulfilment, a degree of reconstruction far more fundamental and far-reaching than the measures properly called 'reforms' which our Victorian ancestors achieved in their days of greatness. But that there is a close kinship between our own times and theirs is suggested by the cry uttered by Tennyson in that most completely mid-Victorian of poems, 'In Memoriam':

> I falter where I firmly trod,
>   And, falling with my weight of cares
>   Upon the great world's altar-stairs,
> That slope through darkness up to God,
>
> I stretch lame hands of faith, and grope
>   And gather dust and chaff, and call
>   To what I feel is Lord of all,
> And faintly trust the larger hope.

1. In *Equality* (1949) the present writer has attempted to trace some of the origins of the modern 'social service State' in Britain.

MINISTRIES, 1815–1914

Party	Date Formed	Prime Minister	Chancellor of Exchequer	Foreign Secretary
T	June, 1812	Lord Liverpool	N. Vansittart (From January, 1823, F. J. Robinson)	Lord Castlereagh (From September, 1822, George Canning)
T	April, 1827	George Canning	George Canning	Lord Dudley
T	September, 1827	Lord Goderich	J. C. Herries	Lord Dudley
T	January, 1828	Duke of Wellington	H. Goulburn	Lord Dudley (From June, 1828, Lord Aberdeen)
W	November, 1830	Lord Grey	Lord Althorp	Lord Palmerston
W	July, 1834	Lord Melbourne	Lord Althorp	Lord Palmerston
C	December, 1834	Sir Robert Peel	Sir Robert Peel	Duke of Wellington
W	April, 1835	Lord Melbourne	T. Spring Rice (From August, 1839, Sir F. T. Baring)	Lord Palmerston
C	September, 1841	Sir Robert Peel	H. Goulburn	Lord Aberdeen
W	July, 1846	Lord J. Russell	Sir C. Wood	Lord Palmerston (From December, 1851, Lord Granville)
C	February, 1852	Lord Derby	B. Disraeli	Lord Malmesbury
Coalition	December, 1852	Lord Aberdeen	W. E. Gladstone	Lord J. Russell (From February, 1853, Lord Clarendon)
W	February, 1855	Lord Palmerston	W. E. Gladstone (From Feburary, 1855, Sir G. Cornewall Lewis)	Lord Clarendon
C	February, 1858	Lord Derby	B. Disraeli	Lord Malmesbury
W-L	June, 1859	Lord Palmerston	W. E. Gladstone	Lord J. Russell
W-L	October, 1865	Lord Russell	W. E. Gladstone	Lord Clarendon
C	June, 1866	Lord Derby	B. Disraeli	Lord Stanley
C	Feb... 1868	B. D...	G. W...	

		W. E. Gladstone		
L		(From August, 1873, W. E. Gladstone)	R. Lowe (From August, 1873, W. E. Gladstone)	(From June, 1870, Lord Granville)
C	February, 1874	B. Disraeli (became Lord Beaconsfield, August, 1876)	Sir Stafford Northcote	Lord Derby (From April, 1878, Lord Salisbury)
L	April, 1880	W. E. Gladstone	W. E. Gladstone (From December, 1882, H. C. E. Childers)	Lord Granville
C	June, 1885	Lord Salisbury	Sir M. Hicks Beach	Lord Salisbury
L	February, 1886	W. E. Gladstone	Sir W. V. Harcourt	Lord Rosebery
C	August, 1886	Lord Salisbury	Lord Randolph Churchill (From January, 1887, G. J. Goschen)	Lord Iddesleigh (From January, 1887, Lord Salisbury)
L	August, 1892	W. E. Gladstone	Sir W. V. Harcourt	Lord Rosebery
L	March, 1894	Lord Rosebery	Sir W. V. Harcourt	Lord Kimberley
C	June, 1895	Lord Salisbury	Sir M. Hicks Beach	Lord Salisbury (From October, 1900, Lord Lansdowne)
C	July, 1902	A. J. Balfour	C. T. Ritchie (From May, 1903, Austen Chamberlain)	Lord Lansdowne
L	December, 1905	Sir H. Campbell-Bannerman	H. H. Asquith	Sir Edward Grey
L	April, 1908	H. H. Asquith	D. Lloyd George	Sir Edward Grey

It may be noted from the above that the century 1815–1914, which spans six reigns, includes thirty Ministries; that exactly half these Ministries were headed by members of the House of Commons, half by members of the House of Lords; that throughout the century the Chancellor of the Exchequer was always a Commoner; that Sir Edward Grey was the first Foreign Secretary since Canning who was not a peer, although both Lord John Russell and Lord Palmerston were members of the House of Commons. Five of the Prime Ministers previously held office as Chancellors of the Exchequer, five previously held office as Foreign Secretary. The total period is almost exactly equally divided between years of Tory-Conservative and years of Whig-Liberal rule.

T = Tory; W = Whig; C = Conservative; L = Liberal

SUGGESTED BOOKS

THE reader who wishes to pursue further the more important aspects of nineteenth-century history discussed in the text should find the following suggestions useful.

A. *General*

The best up-to-date account of the period as a whole is given in two volumes of the *Oxford History of England*. They are E. L. Woodward: *The Age of Reform (1815–1870)* and R. C. K. Ensor: *England, 1870–1914*. A more detailed general history is the great French classic, Élie Halévy: *A History of the English People*. It covers the years 1815–52 and 1895–1915 only, and its six volumes have all been translated into English by E. I. Watkin. The first and fifth volumes have been published as Pelican Books. Shorter general surveys are J. R. M. Butler: *A History of England, 1815–1918*, and G. M. Trevelyan: *British History in the Nineteenth Century* (1782–1901). G. M. Young: *Portrait of an Age* is a masterly bird's-eye view, but none too easy for the general reader to follow.

B. *Particular aspects*

The standard authority on the economic history of the period is J. H. Clapham: *An Economic History of Modern Britain*, of which the first volume covers the years 1820–1850, the second 1850–1886, and the third 1886–1914. Though immensely detailed it is less formidable to read than it seems. L. H. Jenks: *The Migration of British Capital to 1875* deals brilliantly with the financial growth of Britain: L. C. A. Knowles: *The Industrial and Commercial Revolutions in Great Britain*, with the revolutions of machinery and transport.

Political and constitutional history is, as usual, well covered in a multitude of books. A. V. Dicey: *Law and Public Opinion in England* is a classical examination of legislative reforms. K. B. Smellie: *A Hundred Years of English Government* traces the relations between social and political movements and administrative changes. Social and political movements as such are dealt with in Mark Hovell: *The Chartist Movement;* G. D. H. Cole: *British Working Class Politics, 1832–1914;* J. L. and B. Hammond: *The Bleak Age* (Pelican Book, 1947); Norman Gash: *Politics in the Age of Peel;* George Dangerfield: *The Strange Death of Liberal England;* W. S. Adams: *Edwardian Heritage.*

Religion and cultural developments may be studied in L. E. Elliott-Binns: *Religion in the Victorian Era;* J. W. Adamson: *English Education, 1789–1902;* H. Wickham Steed: *The Press* (Penguin Special); D. C. Somervell: *English Thought in the Nineteenth Century;* Holbrook Jackson: *The Eighteen Nineties* (Pelican Book).

C. *Biographies*

Biographies of nineteenth-century public figures are legion. See the detailed bibliographies in Woodward and Ensor (mentioned above). But it may be worth pointing out that the standard biography of *Gladstone* by John Morley and that of *Disraeli* by Monypenny and Buckle have been conveniently condensed into *Disraeli and Gladstone,* by D. C. Somervell. H. Bolitho: *The Reign of Queen Victoria,* is an excellent narrative biography covering the main part of the century. The *Autobiography* of J. S. Mill offers unique insight into the extension and modifications of Benthamism, as well as into the personality of one of the era's greatest men.

D. *Contemporary works*

The novels of Charles Dickens, Anthony Trollope, and H. G. Wells offer the most attractive way into the 'atmosphere' of the period; Walter Bagehot's *The English Constitution* and *Lombard Street* are shrewd contemporary comments; and Matthew Arnold's *Culture and Anarchy* is one of the best examples of Victorian self-criticism. The poems of Lord Tennyson are a remarkably complete expression of the problems and spirit of Victorian England.

INDEX

*Some other Pelican books
are described on the
remaining pages*

The History of the British Navy

MICHAEL LEWIS

A 400

In attempting a connected story of that great Service which
has been through the centuries the first, and often the last,
line of British defence, and the spearhead of Britain's
expansion when the time came, Professor Lewis has tried
to put the Royal Navy into its true perspective in history
in general and sea-history in particular. He shows its origin
in the Crown's personal sea-force, still blended with, and
largely reliant upon, the Country's total sea-force, and
relates how it emerged as the principal fighting element
in her sea-strength: principal, but not only, fighting
element, because the natural reserves of the Royal Navy
are, and always have been, an integral part of the *whole*
Navy. The book develops chronologically, showing not
only how the Navy – all of it – grew up, but also why it
grew and, in its growth, what benefits it conferred upon
the Country which it was created to serve. There are thus
three interwoven strands – a Naval History, following, in
such detail as space allows, the work and actions of the
Service, and how they affected British policy as a whole;
a History of the Royal Navy itself, showing its birth and
development in ships, men, weapons, etc., and – its
corollary – a History of its age-old Reserves, once the
parents from which it sprang – the Royal Naval Reserve
and the Royal Naval Volunteer Reserve.

The Ancient Civilizations of Peru

J. ALDEN MASON

A395

Our detailed knowledge of the peoples of pre-Columbian Peru has grown enormously since 1940. Many expeditions have made excavations and published their reports. Regions archaeologically unknown hitherto have yielded their secrets, and far more is known of all of them. Especially is this true of the cultures that preceded the Inca whom Pizarro found and conquered in one of the great adventures of history. Four thousand years before his day, radiocarbon analyses now permit us to state with confidence, simple fishermen-hunters on the coast were beginning the long climb toward the extraordinary blend of communism and monarchy that was the Inca empire. Our concepts of the latter and of its history also have been altered somewhat by recent studies. This book presents a summary of our present knowledge and point of view regarding the development and nature of these past civilizations and their fascinating and diversified country.